The Bernonville Affair

Other books you may enjoy from this publisher:

The Empty Cathedral, by Jean-Paul Lefebvre
Zen & the Art of Post-Modern Canada, by Stephen Schecter
The Last Cod Fish, by Pol Chantraine
No Mud on the Back Seat, by Gerald Clark
*A Canadian Myth: Quebec, between Canada and the
Illusion of Utopia,* by William Johnson
Economics in Crisis, by Louis-Philippe Rochon
Dead-End Democracy?, by Yves Leclerc
Voltaire's Man in America, by Jean-Paul de Lagrave
Moral Panic: Biopolitics Rising, by John Fekete
The Making of a Spy, by Gordon Lunan

CANADIAN CATALOGUING IN PUBLICATION DATA

Lavertu, Yves

The Bernonville Affair: a French war criminal in post-WWII Québec

Includes bibliographical references; includes bibliography; includes chronology

ISBN 1-895854-41-5

To receive our current catalogue and be kept on our mailing list for announcements of new titles, send your name and address to:

*Robert Davies Publishing,
P.O. Box 702, Outremont, Quebec, Canada H2V 4N6*

Yves Lavertu

The
Bernonville
Affair:

a French war criminal in post-WWII Québec

translated from French by George Tombs

Robert Davies Publishing
MONTREAL—TORONTO—PARIS

ISBN 1-895854-41-5

This book may be ordered in Canada from
General Distribution Services,

☎1-800-387-0141 / 1-800-387-0172 FAX 1-416-445-5967;

in the U.S.A., from Associated Publishers Group,
1501 County Hospital Road, Nashville, TN 37218
dial toll-free 1-800-327-5113;

or call the publisher, toll-free throughout North America,

1-800-481-2440, FAX 1-514-481-9973;

In the UK, order from Drake International Services,
Market House, Market Place, Deddington, Oxford OX15 OSF
Telephone/Fax 01869 338240

The publisher takes this opportunity to thank the
Canada Council and the *Ministère de la Culture du Québec*
for their continuing support.

Table of Contents

Preface by André Malavoy 9
Author's Foreword 15

CHAPTER ONE
The survivor of Saint Pacôme 19

CHAPTER II
Pétain's Quebec 31

CHAPTER III
The fugitives 46

CHAPTER IV
A provincial affair 57

CHAPTER V
A national affair 74

CHAPTER VI
Obeying a legitimate government 92

Chapter VII
A new Riel affair? 117

CONCLUSION
Quebec-family-fatherland 137

Chronology & Bibliography 147

Index 155

PREFACE

B etween 1951 and 1956, I enjoyed a privileged position in Quebec, due in large part to the fact that France's official representation at the time was completely inadequate. During this period, I approached just about all the members of the local intelligentsia, some of whom even became my close friends. As a result, I believe I am well-placed to comment on their opinions about Pétain and the Collaboration, or at least on what they let me know about their opinions.

When France's Commissioner General of Tourism, a renowned veteran of the Resistance, sent me to Canada in June 1951, he told me, "you are going to be swept up in the whirlwind of the Bernonville affair. Do not consider yourself bound by the tradition of diplomatic discretion. You should frankly express your views." In any case, that is what I would have done.

I wanted to act in Quebec as a witness for France. I spoke about the recent drama of the German Occupation, of the Vichy régime, of the Resistance. Over and over again, I told my largely still-Pétainist audience that the Vichy régime was one of the most shameful episodes of the history of France, that the honour of the country, and indeed its salvation, were without any doubt to be found on the side of Charles de Gaulle and the Resistance. I have to say that the people I engaged in conversation very rarely sought to defend Pétain in my presence.

I believe that in general, a large majority of decision-makers and intellectuals in Quebec in those days had supported the Vichy régime. Indeed, in the after-war years, they continued to have a certain admiration for Vichy. Others, meanwhile, had had the good sense to support de Gaulle and the Resistance.

"The world will be saved by a handful of men" — those are the profound words of André Gide. In France, the majority, at least the majority in the non-occupied zone, lined up behind Pétain. Bernanos wrote of the first Free French forces to rally to de Gaulle: "we were a handful of men, in desperate circumstances, motivated by honour." The change of heart of the majority in France began in 1942. Quebec was not as well-informed or as involved, and did not experience this change of heart. Indeed, I saw how the pro-Vichy ideology carried on in Quebec after the war. This ideology was fed in 1944 and 1945 by the excesses that were committed in France during the purges that followed the liberation of French soil from German forces and the collapse of the Vichy regime. It is important to recognize that there were many grave excesses. It is crucial to understand that the legitimate rage of the people was very hard to control. These excesses were skillfully exploited by Canadian Pétainists.

Considering my unceasing condemnation of Vichy and Marshal Pétain, and my constant pleas in favor of de Gaulle and the Resistance, very few people actually sought to contradict me. The most frequent response to my criticism of the failings of the Vichy régime was: "we didn't know." To which I replied: "but you ought to have known."

I can classify into three categories the reactions of my Canadian friends and acquaintances to my positions. A first group was made up of those who never contradicted what I said, even if their position had been and possibly still was the opposite of my own. Which proves that they had a guilty conscience. I am convinced that some of them had changed their mind, however, even if the words never passed their lips. Among these people, I would include Roger Duhamel and the late actor Doris Lussier.

In a second category were those who sought to defend Vichy in my presence; for example René Chaloult; and Camillien Houde, who was my guest on several occasions and whom I also visited in his office at City Hall. One time, when I told him point-blank what he should think of the respective values of de Gaulle and Pétain, he gave me a typically Norman answer: "peut-être bien" — "well, that could be."

The third category is more interesting. It is made up of those who were seduced by Vichy during the war, and who publicly changed their minds afterward. I believe that I played some part in their change of heart. I invoked a wide range of arguments, among them my own personal experience, and never stopped denouncing the dubious conduct of Marshal Pétain. Beneath his impressive appearance lay the reality of his crimes and the shame of the collaboration with Hitler. I added that the opposition of Quebec nationalists to conscription, which was supposedly a healthy reaction to the dominant position of English-Canadians, struck me not only as an error, but also as an act of cowardice. By campaigning against conscription, people refused to become involved in a clear-cut cause of justice. And while these people constantly proclaimed their devotion to France, in fact they betrayed her.

I frequented the company of the journalist and well-known public figure André Laurendeau for many years. Jean-Marc Léger, brother of Cardinal Léger and later on a diplomat, introduced him to me as soon as I arrived, remarking moreover that I had a special task to perform in Laurendeau's case. While Jean-Marc Léger had been a Pétainist, his views about Vichy had substantially evolved by the time we met. I do believe that I fully opened his eyes to the shame of the Vichy régime. However, I do not believe I did any more than budge him slightly, when it came to the 1942 conscription affair.

Jean-Marc Léger had just returned from France, where he had been deeply affected by what he had seen and heard. I think I won him completely over to the ideal of the Resistance and to an admiration for de Gaulle. From that point onward, his work both as a journalist and a radio host reflected this change. No Quebecker was more Gaullist than he. Consequently, I find it regrettable to document here the fleeting error of his younger years, which only consisted in writing three letters offering his services to Bernonville. When Jean-Marc Léger learned the truth, he came over to the right side, once and for all. Before, during and after Charles de Gaulle's historic visit to Quebec in 1967, Jean-Marc Léger was one of his most faithful and courageous defenders.

RELIGIOUS SUPPORT FOR BERNONVILLE

It seems certain that some religious communities offered refuge and help to the traitor Bernonville and many other people who compromised themselves with Vichy and the Germans (the close relationship between the two is there for all to see). This was shown for example by the Touvier affair. The same sort of collusion (and in such cases, help can only be called collusion), intensified by the clerical nature of society, could also be found in postwar Quebec.

But it would be unjust and wrong to turn this observation into an antireligious polemic. A distinction should be drawn between help and refuge. Help is worth condemning. But refuge corresponds to a centuries-old tradition of the monastic life, which sees a duty in welcoming the person seeking refuge, without knowing who he is or what he has done. The same welcome is reserved for all men, regardless of their political positions. Because of circumstances after the war, this refuge was above all sought by former collaborators and traitors. If these same

11

people had claimed to be on the opposite side, they would no doubt have been welcomed in just the same way.

It is worth condemning cases where active help was offered, however. More than one case cropped up in France immediately after the war; many more cases cropped up in Quebec. To understand how that could have occurred, one has to remember that the Catholic Church in Quebec was far more interested in defending its privileges than in working for the Christian faith.

In judging the French clergy, one has also to remember the many cases where Resistance fighters found refuge — and not only refuge but very often active help. I may be partisan, but I sincerely believe we should pay tribute to this help.

The cause of the Resistance was not unjust; it was a struggle for honour and liberty. At best, people supported Vichy out of weakness, at worst, too often, out of treachery. What was particularly grave about the Pétain régime was the way it created ambiguity about the defence of traditional values and submission to the hateful laws of Nazism. Because of this ambiguity, great numbers of people were led astray, in Quebec as well as in France.

Nobody can deny the sad fact that there was collusion between Vichy on the one hand and a considerable portion of the French bourgeoisie and Catholic Church on the other. In the Church itself, the upper clergy were the most affected. But an important fact is often left out of judgments of French reactions to the Occupation, whether through ignorance or deliberately. Yes, there were bishops blessing the Marshal, but priests took part in the struggle of the Resistance more than any other single class of society. The statistics clearly demonstrate that the proportion of priests deported or shot by the Germans was ten times higher than their proportion in the general population. Among these thousands of examples, I will cite two: General de Bénouville[1], dropped by parachute in France after D-Day, found refuge in a convent where the Mother Superior hid his secret orders underneath a statue of the Blessed Virgin. And it was in the visiting room of a convent in Pont-l'Abbé, in Brittany, that I made contact in 1941 with the intelligence network of the French Underground, a network which I later ran.

We should be wary of manichean judgments, such as the one that places the Resistance on the left, among the working classes, and places the Collaboration on the right, among the bourgeoisie and the clergy. The truth is far, far more complex in France, as indeed it was in

Germany. In Germany, we should not forget there was widespread popular support for Hitler (whose movement was rightly called national-socialist), while the German Resistance was largely rooted in the aristocracy and among military officers. In France, we should recall that an overwhelming majority of the National Assembly of the "Front Populaire" accorded full powers to Pétain. The first people to join the Resistance and rally to de Gaulle were mainly in the upper bourgeoisie and nationalist aristocracy, which were right-wing classes. That is clearly shown by General de Gaulle's first entourage.

Very quickly, however, de Gaulle received broad popular support, above all in occupied France. Without that kind of popular support, no movement has a hope of taking root. An example: once Soviet Russia entered World War II, the French Communists were able to mobilize a considerable proportion of the people. As for de Gaulle, he wished to remain above all parties. He embodied France as a whole. I do not believe anyone else has embodied his country to the same extent. That is surely the reason why Quebeckers later welcomed him with such extraordinary warmth. Many Quebeckers are distrustful of the French — often, admittedly, with reason — but when they faced de Gaulle, they faced not simply a Frenchman, but France herself.

André Malavoy[2]
June 1994

NOTES

1. A peculiar coincidence. On the one hand, a representative of the treacherous aristocracy, Bernonville; on the other, of the heroic aristocracy, Bénouville. There were far more cases like Bénouville than like Bernonville.

2. André Malavoy was one of the handful of French citizens who responded immediately to General de Gaulle's call to arms on June 18, 1940. He arrived in Quebec in the summer of 1951, and became a personal friend of André Laurendeau. From 1959 to 1992, he was president of the Association des Français Libres of Montreal.

FOREWORD[1]

"...It is dreadful to think that history will be written only by our enemies."[2]

So wrote one man in his seventies, to another man of roughly the same age, in 1968. Writing the words was Jacques Dugé de Bernonville, a man of action. Reading them was Robert Rumilly, an ideologue. The two men could see the story of their struggle only in the bleakest manichean terms. In this account of the "Bernonville affair," I do not intend to take a position, either for them or against them. Nor do I seek to judge these men by the standards of the past (let alone of the present). The awesome task I am taking on in this book is to treat the subject with scrupulous fairness.

The book springs from two experiences. The first is my sustained interest, for close to ten years, in France's wartime Vichy régime. Fueling that interest are the resounding echoes of General de Gaulle's celebrated cry in Montreal in 1967 — "Vive le Québec libre!" — as well as a fascination for a period in French history when every person was confronted with tough choices.

As for the second experience, it is rooted in the accidental discovery, in December 1993, of a historical source revealing the extent of the relationship between Quebec and Pétainism. Quite by chance, I came across the Robert Rumilly papers in the Archives Nationales du Québec in Montreal. I quickly recognized the importance of these documents in helping to understand a phenomenon and a political affair which are practically non-existent in contemporary Quebec's collective memory.

Rumilly (the well-known quasi-official historian of Québec Premier Maurice Duplessis) had accumulated a heap of letters, telegrams, and newspaper clippings about this case, possibly in order to return one day to tell his tale, or perhaps as a posthumous gift to other historians.[3]

Throughout my research, I have sought above all to take an uncompromising and historiographical look at the events described in this book. The reader will note that few people have been interviewed. To some, that may seem questionable. But it was the only method enabling me to plough through the documents and still keep a clear head. I chose to adopt this method, because writing a work of instant history is a very precarious exercise, given the fact that Quebec's current

15

political situation is in a state of flux. At the same time,I want to make clear that the quotations to be found in this book have been reprinted in their entirety, regardless of what I may have preferred to publish and sometimes even running counter to my own views.

My task has been mainly to describe in a rather conventional way an event (or rather a series of events) related to an affair that was front-page news over a three-year period. As a piece of historical writing, this book seems far-removed from the École des Annales, the school of historical writing I identified with during my years at university. In this book, the reader will find no analysis of a deep current, or even of a surface wave. Instead, he will find at most the straightforward description of foam at the surface, if I am allowed this analogy.

I have tried to make a leap into micro-history. Given my background as a journalist, it is natural for me to take a ground-level look at certain facts and actions. My approach has consisted in reconstituting the whole range of possibilities facing an individual, at a given moment in his life story. Relatively few individuals are identified by name.

However, this book of micro-history has meaning only insofar as it associates those individuals with the communities that were concerned with the Bernonville affair. From the multitude of individual actions arises the context at the heart of the affair. Indeed, the Bernonville affair can be interpreted as a microcosm of an entire dimension of Quebec's recent political history.

In developing this approach, I have benefited from the works of many historians who have changed our perceptions of Vichy over the last few decades. I am deeply indebted to them.

This little book does not claim to be a monograph on the relationship between Pétain and Quebec. If anything, this book merely sketches the outlines of that relationship. One hopes that historians will soon apply themselves to filling this gap in our historical knowledge of Quebec. This work has a more limited objective: that of grouping together the most important facts about the Bernonville affair. It should be noted *all* the facts may not be presented here. Other facts, other names will be turned up by other researchers, whose work may be already under way or perhaps not yet begun. As for the interpretations offered in this book, they will no doubt be confronted with other interpretations as our understanding unfolds over the years to come.

May I add that I am pleased that the english-speaking public now has access to a chapter of Quebec history in whose web, during that time, various English Canadians were enmeshed. The decision to publish the translation was an initiative of Robert Davies Publishing, and to them and the translator, Mr. George Tombs, must devolve the responsability for the final english text.

Let me say in closing that I hope this book will be perceived not as a polemical attack, but rather as a work of historical explanation, a disturbing one at that.

Finally, I would like to offer my sincere thanks to the following people: the group of veterans of the Free French forces in Montreal, Jacques Charpentier, Roland Haumont and André Malavoy. They provided me with the benefit of their indispensable experience in the field as well as their knowledge both of Jacques Dugé de Bernonville's past and of Quebec support for Pétain, both before and during the period under study. Roland Haumont and André Malavoy have moreover kindly read the manuscript.

My thanks also go to Sol Littman of the Simon Wiesenthal Centre in Toronto. His great knowledge of the Bernonville affair and of the possible ways of interpreting it have helped me throughout my research. I would also like to thank Lise Bissonnette, publisher of the daily newspaper *Le Devoir*, for reading the manuscript and sharing her reactions with me. The same goes for Jean-François Nadeau, a doctoral student in political science at the Université de Montréal. An old hand at reading theses, he saw the text just before its publication in French, and sent his remarks along.

I must also mention the vital contribution of Adrienne Courcy, Rolande Plourde and Raymond-Marie Gagnon for patiently reconstructing the time that Jacques de Bernonville spent in St. Pacôme, in the Lower St. Lawrence region.

A few people helped correct the manuscript. Among them, I would like to thank the Weedon reading committee as well as Corinne Haumont. I would like to thank those who helped me outside of the purvey of my research work. Christiane Samuel, Luc Dupont and many others too numerous to mention stimulated me with their encouragement and discussions. Even though I do not name them all here, I owe them a lot.

All of the above-mentioned people have helped a great deal, but are not in any way responsible for errors of fact, dates or of interpretation which may have slipped into the book. Such errors, of course, are entirely my own.

YVES LAVERTU

June 1994

FOOTNOTES

1. Notes concerning abbreviations:

Robert Rumilly Collection, Archives nationales du Québec in Montreal, box 14: RR; ANQ; 14.

Louis Saint Laurent Collection, National Archives of Canada in Ottawa: LST; ANC.

Bernonville Collection, National Archives of Canada in Ottawa: DB; ANC.

Bernonville File, Archives of the Canadian Jewish Congress in Montreal: Db; ACJC.

2. Letter from Jacques de Bernonville (Rio de Janeiro, Brazil) to Robert Rumilly, February 7, 1968 (RR; ANQ; 12).

3. The Rumilly papers are a crucial part of an ongoing revision of interpretations of the recent past. Interested readers should consult the following: Gonzalo Arriaga and Jean-François Nadeau, "Maréchal, nous voilà!", *Le Devoir*, May 20, 1994; Bernard Plante, "Filière québécoise pour criminels de guerre", *Le Devoir*, May 21, 1994; Stéphane Baillargeon, "Duplessis, nous voilà!", *Le Devoir*, May 26, 1994; Jean-Marc Léger, "Un scoop manqué", *Le Devoir* May 26, 1994; Lise Bissonnette, "Envisager le passé", *Le Devoir*, May 27, 1994; Gonzalo Arriaga and Jean-François Nadeau, "La raison et les passions", *Le Devoir* June 3, 1994; Béatrice Richard et Francis Simard, "Blessures de guerre", *Le Devoir*, June 9, 1994.

CHAPTER ONE

The survivor of Saint Pacôme

E very evening after work, a nondescript office employee named Jacques Benoit went to the Saint Pacôme, Québec post office. Under his one good arm he carried the same mail as usual, and once this scar-faced man finished sending his mail, he returned to his room at the Bon Accueil Hotel.

A practiced eye could discern something military in the gait of this foreigner, who replied rather suspiciously when spoken to. It sometimes happened that his brow furrowed suddenly, and his face tightened. Of course, the fact he was partly deaf accounted for this expression. But one also got the feeling that he wanted to stay well out of sight.

Jacques Benoit arrived in Saint-Pacôme-de-Kamouraska in mid-winter, alone, dressed in what people in 1947 called "local garb". At the time, the little village of 3,000 inhabitants nestled close to La Pocatière, a few kilometres inland from the St. Lawrence River, seemed quite prosperous. In the village, a young, still-unknown piano virtuoso named André Gagnon was just entering adolescence, already composing music.

In Saint Pacôme, like in villages everywhere, strangers were the talk of the town. Still, nobody dared ask too many questions about this Frenchman with his curt manner. True enough, he was the protégé of the local seigneur, Alfred Plourde, who along with his brothers bought the St. Pacôme sawmill from the Power Lumber Company a few years beforehand. And when the sawblades were flying, everything seemed right in the world.

The forest, the great provider, was everywhere to be seen, covering the land right down to the Alleghenies, and even in the Ouelle itself, the river winding through the village. In spring, logs cut by the lumberjacks over the winter were flipped into the water and floated down to the sawmill.

Although Jacques Benoit was tall and well-built, he did not work in the lumber camps. His paralyzed arm and education designated him for an office job at Plourde and Bros. Besides, Alfred Plourde planned to treat him with all the consideration due to an important man. The businessman had heard confidential information about Benoit's past from a lawyer friend, Noël Dorion. Just before the Christmas holidays, Dorion asked him to find a job in his company for the French gentleman. Although Benoit was a fugitive, said the lawyer, he was none other than the right-hand man of the great Pétain, ruler of occupied France.

Life appeared to be placid for this immigrant with his foreign ways. He was even preparing to welcome his family, who had remained behind in France. In February and March 1947 Benoit's wife arrived in Saint Pacôme, followed by three of his daughters: Catherine, Josianne and Chantal. The adolescents passed their first Canadian winter skiing on the hills nearby, and found their new life enchanting.

For awhile, the Benoit family lodged with the Dionne sisters, and then moved on to the Bon Accueil Hotel. That is when letters began arriving from France. A young housekeeper tidying up the lodgings one day came across one of the letters, which revealed to her the true identity of the family, but she did not make known her discovery. Still, from then on, she considered that the Benoits were also the *Bernonvilles*.

A COURAGEOUS SOLDIER

Jacques Dugé de Bernonville was born in Auteuil, near Paris, in 1897. Born into a well-to-do aristocratic family,[1] the young boy was immersed in Catholicism from an early age. The Jesuits took care of him and he owed to this formative period of his life the habit of never missing morning mass.

World War One gave him the opportunity to prove his real physical courage, and he was quickly named lieutenant of the Chasseurs Alpins. His bravery was recognized, and he received many decorations, among them the Croix de Guerre. After the war, he pursued a brilliant military career, serving in Syria during the Druze uprising. He was awarded the Légion d'Honneur.[2]

It was during this period that he developed his political ideas. In 1926, Count Dugé de Bernonville was an active member of the Action Française, a group headed by the Fascist ideologue Charles Maurras. In this agitated post-war setting, he got to know people who favoured the restoration of the monarchy and an authoritarian style of government. That same year, he was arrested for being involved in a royalist plot.

On returning to civilian life in the 1930s, Bernonville got even more deeply involved in the extreme right-wing movement. He really wanted to do damage to the Communists. In January 1938, he was implicated in the plot to overthrow the Republic by force, an incident that has gone down in history as the Cagoule Plot.[3] He was imprisoned once again, but was released several months later on account of a lack of evidence.

At the outbreak of World War Two, Bernonville was called up once again to command the Chasseurs Alpins. But the rapid collapse of France in the spring of 1940 and above all the installation of the Pétain régime led him along a completely new path. All things considered, it was a quite natural path for him to follow, given his political convictions. As soon as the Third Republic was pronounced dead and the country was split into two zones, he joined the Vichy régime, which controlled the southern zone of France — the zone not yet occupied by the Germans.

At first, he was involved in youth organizations. Then, along with a former colleague from the Action Française, Abel Bonnard, he helped set up the Légion Française des Combattants, the breeding ground of several collaborationist organizations which got closer and closer to the Germans.

On October 18, 1941, Count de Bernonville, his wife and their four children left Marseilles for North Africa. Their destination was Morocco, where the former officer had been appointed chargé d'affaires for Jewish Questions. Bernonville answered to the Commission for Jewish Questions, which had been set up to implement recent anti-Semitic legislation, in both France and its territories. Among the laws passed by Vichy was the October 1940 law on the Status of Jews, the first step leading to their exclusion from the social, political and economic life of France.[4]

21

After a brief stay in France in the summer of 1942, where he met his new boss, Louis Darquier de Pellepoix [5], Bernonville left once more for Morocco. There he continued to take part in the social exclusion of Jews, and also helped set up the Légion du Service d'Ordre Légionnaire (SOL). Ultimately, this organization would compromise itself by delivering intelligence which ended up in the hands of the Germans.

Then, in Fall 1942, three weeks before the Anglo-American landing in North Africa, Bernonville and his family left Morocco for Paris, where Bernonville took up quarters at 12, place Malesherbes, in order to organize the Phalange Africaine. This new movement was ferociously anti-Communist, and signed up French recruits determined to fight the English in North Africa.[6] From his base in Paris, Bernonville acted as secretary-general. At this time, he established his first contacts with people from the SD, the *Sicherheitsdienst* or German security service. In actual fact, Bernonville didn't achieve much with the Phalange Africaine. The creation of the Milice on January 31, 1943 came at a convenient time for Bernonville. From this date onward, there were no longer grounds for doubt: Bernonville had crossed the borderline between State collaboration, as practiced by the Vichy government, and direct ideological collaboration with the Nazis themselves. He had become a collaborator.

A CAJUN FOR COLLEGE DIRECTOR

The Milice was fully supported by the Vichy régime. Headed by Joseph Darnand, a former member of the Cagoule, the Milice was conceived as a vast movement of Vichy's "National Revolution" bringing together the most extreme collaborators. Bernonville was Catholic, monarchist and anti-Bolshevist, and thus saw the Milice as the simple extension of his involvement in the right-wing causes of Maurras. He joined willingly and in the company of many notable people, reactionaries and nationalists, some of whom were even sometimes hostile to Germany. Others like him, members of old noble families, then began joining: de Bourmont, de Vaugelas, de La Rochefoucauld, de la Noüe du Vair.

In the Winter of 1943, the latter was appointed director of the Milice officer's college in Saint-Martin d'Uriage[7]. As director of studies, Bernonville acted as one of his lieutenants. The atmosphere and day-to-day life at the château have been very well described by Jacques

Delperrié de Bayac, author of a unique, ground-breaking work on the Milice.[8]

Du Vair was a feudal sort of man, an American of Acadian parentage who took the first ship across the Atlantic to defend France as soon as war broke out. His grandfather was well-established in America, yet had served in the Franco-Prussian War of 1870. His father showed just the same sort of loyalty to France during World War One.

Du Vair himself — this Cajun, royalist and specialist in the philosophy of Thomas Aquinas — loved France unconditionally. One of the favorite pastimes of this Catholic mystic concerned the fate of Canada. He liked to say that one day Canada would become France's once again. The reason was straightforward, he thought: French Canadians have more children than "les Anglais" — English Canadians.

There was also something conspiratorial in du Vair's nostalgic personality. During the summer of 1943, du Vair got Bernonville and other disciples involved in an attempted coup d'État to overthrow Vichy and restore the monarchy. Once Darnand got wind of plans for the putsch, a truly medieval scene took place, in which the head of the Milice laid siege to the barricaded château. Darnand finally won out, and du Vair was thrown out of the Milice.

As for Bernonville, he somehow managed to escape the wrath of Darnand. And like Darnand, he pledged allegiance to Hitler in Fall 1943. From that date onward, he was on the payroll of the 9th Brandebourg regiment[9] of the Waffen SS, with enrolment number 605[10].

ON THE PLÂTEAU DE GLIÈRES AND IN THE VERCORS REGION

For his role in the attack on the Resistance on the plâteau de Glières, Bernonville obtained a full pardon from Darnand. In early 1944, the forces of repression began rolling into Annecy in Upper Savoy. With those forces was Bernonville, who had been ordered to command a contingent of the Milice. The members of the Milice were now armed and gathered together under the banner of the 2nd unit of the Franc-Garde. Joseph Darnand was now a full member of the Vichy government and running the operations of the Maintenance of Order.[11]

A few months beforehand, the local prefect sounded the alarm by warning there was a large concentration of Maquis fighters in the region. Among the members of the local Vichy administration was the chief physician at the Annecy hospital, Georges Montel, a man who would have a chance to get to know Bernonville at a later date and in another place.

The arrival of Vichy forces meant that the Resistance fighters, who were awaiting an airdrop of supplies, had to adopt the new strategy of digging in. Colonel Romans-Petit gave Tom Morel the mission of taking a detachment to to an altitude of 1500 metres on the plâteau of Glières, where they would have to await parachute drops.[12]

Marshal Pétain and Pierre Laval wanted the repression of the Resistance fighters to be well-handled. For the time being, the forces of the police and the Milice would do little more than surround the 465 Resistance fighters.

Bernonville was nevertheless active. A few weeks later, one of his men, Claude Maubourguet, gave an account to the collaborationist weekly *Je suis partout* of his own role in the repression at Bernonville's side. For Maubourguret, Bernonville was one of the finest soldiers serving in the revolution currently underway:

> "Relentlessly, he conducts patrols, visits the outposts, reconnoiters. He is to be found everywhere; in his old jalopy, he crisscrosses the area... And his tall and gaunt silhouette, and his white jacket marked with the insignia of his infantry battalion, have made him popular throughout the region.

> "When I enter the room, he is bent over the ordnance survey map. He studies it a moment. Then he gives the alarm: enemy units are trying to infiltrate our positions. As soon as I arrive, there is already a chance of doing battle."[13]

Bernonville often repeated the same phrase to his troops as they tracked down the Resistance: "Aim well, but fire without hatred, for these are our brothers."[14]

The forces of the Maintenance of Order were being held in check, so the Germans decided to intervene vigorously. Darnand managed to have some of his units included in the assault planned for March 26th. On that Sunday, three German battalions, along with 400 men of the German police and the SS, as well as units of the Milice commanded by de Bourmont and Dagostini, smashed the Resistance to pieces. A few days beforehand, the Resistance leader, Tom Morel, had been killed. Ultimately, the 465 Maquis fighters managed to hold out for eight weeks.

Once again, the forces of the Milice played a role, by trapping the Maquis fighters who sought to escape. Like the other commanders, Bernonville ordered his Milice units to mop up the Resistance. Of the men tracked down and trapped, 180 were captured. Pétain and Laval recommended that moderate measures be taken during the repression. But those men suspected of being Communists were tortured and executed. Philippe Henriot crowed victory on Radio-Paris, and blasted the "terrorists" of the Resistance once more.

Now that the Resistance on the plateau de Glières had been wiped out, Commander de Bernonville took in hand the repression of the Vercors region. At the beginning of April 1944, he arrived in Chapelle-en-Vercors, a little village near Grenoble, followed by a convoy of trucks transporting members of the Milice. Under the orders of Bernonville and Dagostini, 500 franc-gardes as well as policemen and mobile troops began operations. On April 16th, a Maquis unit of 90 armed men was attacked around 1600 hours, by a detachment of 250 members of the Milice and members of the Groupe mobile de réserve (GMR). The battle raged all night, and Dugé de Bernonville began mopping up the following morning.

For more than a week, he dealt extremely severely with the villagers in the area. Bernonville and his assistant Dagostini set fire to farms and houses. They made numerous arrests leading to the execution, after torture, of three members of the Resistance. These three men were the pharmacist André Doucin, the farmer Jean-Paul Mially and the postman Casimir Gabriel Ezingeard.

That is when Bernonville's operations in the Vercors came to an end. By July 1944, when the Germans took over once again, he would no longer be in the area. Using gliders, the Germans descended on the 3500 Maquis fighters in order to massacre and disperse them.[15]

TORTURES IN SAONE-ET-LOIRE

In Spring 1944, the terror campaign of the Milice reached a high point. Gangsters and leading citizens had now joined forces in the struggle against Communism. From now to the very end, the Milice and the Nazis were objective allies in a common struggle. According to Delpierré de Bayac, the Milice and the German Nazis shared the same total hatred for Communists, Jews and democrats.

The struggle against the Resistance was intensifying and increasingly taking on the character of a civil war. Although Pétain would later condemn the excesses of the Milice, he claimed on April 28th that the Resistance was compromising the future of the country. Cruelty, torture and summary judgments marked the birth of the Milice's new State.

At the very beginning of May 1944, Jacques de Bernonville took over the role of head of the Maintenance of Order in Burgundy. "Maintaining order" consisted mainly in tracking down Resistance fighters. Burgundy, being in the centre of the country, was of particular strategic importance for the Germans. It was vital to keep a corridor open in the event thousands of soldiers in south and southwest France needed to be evacuated to Germany. At the same time as Bernonville was raging in Burgundy, Guy d'Artois, a Canadian member of the Resistance, was dropped by parachute in April 1944, to install a complex telephone network in the region. All calls made by the Germans were now being intercepted by the Resistance.

Between May 14th and June 25th 1944, Bernonville made 50 arrests in Saône-et-Loire, one of the largest departments in Burgundy. Seven of these people were handed over to the Gestapo, while 38 men and 5 women were imprisoned under detention orders personally signed by Dugé de Bernonville, who had set up his Milice headquarters in Chalon-sur-Saône. Detainees were sometimes delivered to his headquarters, tied to the fender of a car. Bernonville often conducted interrogations, among them that of the garage mechanic Maurice Nedey, who was repeatedly burned and beaten in June.

On June 28th, 1944, Vichy's Secretary of State for Information and Propaganda, Philippe Henriot, was gunned down in Paris by a Resistance commando squad: there were immediate reprisals. Paul Touvier's men hunted down Jews in the area around Lyon. In Mâcon, just to the north of Lyon, members of the Milice assassinated seven people suspected of having contacts with the Resistance. Given the indignation of the local population, the prefect of Saône-et-Loire, Jean-Louis Thoumas, immediately visited Bernonville, who had just been named head of the Maintenance of Order for the Lyon region. Thoumas demanded that measures be taken against the Milice, to assuage the anger of the people, and as a result, Bernonville ordered the arrest of Clavier, departmental head of the Milice for Saône-et-Loire.

Lyon, a city terrorized by Klaus Barbie, was the last French chapter in Bernonville's public career. The Allied landing in Normandy on June 6th marked the beginning of the end of the Nazi Occupation of France. The Milice remained loyal right up to Vichy's last gasp; indeed, the Milice was the only organized force the régime still had. On July 8th, the *Journal officiel* of the French State annonced that three Milice commanders had been awarded the Ordre de la Nation. One of the three was Bernonville.

"The government awards the Ordre de la Nation to: Mr. de Bernonville, head of the permanent Franc-Garde Corps of the French Milice, for the following reasons: particularly energetic Milice commander. Demonstrated, in many operations of the Maintenance of Order in which he was involved, in Upper Savoy, in the Vercors region and in Saône-et-Loire, calm and deliberate courage which already earned him the most laudatory citations in the last two wars. Distinguished himself particularly in Saône-et-Loire where, finding himself cut off with insufficient forces, he succeeded thanks to his efforts to hold down rebellious forces in far greater numbers and to remain in control of the situation." [16]

A little over a month after this episode, around August 20th, Bernonville finally left Lyon for Germany, in the company of senior Nazi officers. He reached Paderborn, headquarters of the 9th Brandebourg.[17] In Paderborn, he took a course to prepare for a sabotage mission behind Allied lines. He was then ordered back to France, to blow up a gas pipeline supplying the American Army as well as the 1st French Army.

In the fall of 1944, Bernonville and three young members of the Milice were parachuted near Melun, as planned.[18] Once the four reached the ground, however, they quickly realized their mission was impossible, and on the first day, they swapped their army fatigues for civilian clothes.

FROM ONE MONASTERY TO ANOTHER

Much like Paul Touvier, Jacques de Bernonville benefited from the support of the Catholic clergy during the Liberation of France. At first, Bernonville simply fled the purges to which he would surely have been subjected if the Resistance had succeeded in tracking him down. In January 1945, in Valence, a warrant for Bernonville's arrest was formally issued: the charge was treason. Then in April 1945, he turned up in a monastery.

The former commander of the Franc-Garde had indeed found refuge in a convent in Upper Savoy. A religious order in Passy took him in and hid him. The community then helped him escape to another monastery, located in the Pyrenees, at Bétharram.[19] This pilgrimage site, situated between Lourdes and the Spanish border, was most likely his last French hiding-place. From there, like many other Vichy supporters, he then crossed into Franco's Spain.

There is no further trace of him until he turned up in November 1946, in New York.[20] Jacques de Bernonville was disguised as a priest now traveling under the name of Jacques Benoit. On November 26th, 1946, after a short stay in New York and after writing to Canadian friends, Benoit left on a Delaware & Hudson train. He reached Canada at the border town of Lacolle, Quebec, dressed as a priest, supplied with forged papers, and told immigration authorities he was a tourist.

On arriving in Canada, he destroyed his forged passport and raced to Quebec City, where he was put up by the well-known restaurant-owner Joseph Kerhulu. Here he met the people he had been writing to, and shortly afterward began work in the office of the Liquor Commission in the Quebec provincial capital. He kept this job until December 1946, when he was offered a new job in Saint-Pacôme-de-Kamouraska, where his host was the businessman and local organizer Alfred Plourde. Mr. Plourde, who was also mayor of Mont-Carmel, invited him over for the weekend at the beginning of 1947. When Benoit arrived, he and Alfred Plourde talked the whole night through about politics and especially about the great Pétain who had by then been interned for a year on Ile d'Yeu, as Alfred's son Roland Plourde recalls.[21] Jacques Benoit quickly recognized that on this side of the Atlantic, influential men such as Plourde were unconditional Pétainists. Joseph Darnand, Bernonville's leader and comrade in arms, executed in October 1945, meant nothing at all to Quebeckers. But Pétain was another story altogether.

FOOTNOTES

1. Bernonville's father was a hydrographic engineer with the Marine nationale and a graduate of Polytechnique.

2. Reconstituting the main events in Jacques de Bernonville's life up to 1946 was done by bringing together four sources: 1) interviews conducted in Spring 1994 with Roland Haumont a Free French veteran living in Montreal since 1950; 2) the indispensable book by Jacques Delpierré de Bayac, *Histoire de la Milice (1918-1945)*, Paris, Fayard, 1969; 3) the in-depth article by McKenzie Porter published by *Maclean's* magazine on

November 15, 1951; 4) the facts exposed by the Toulouse court of justice on January 22, 1949 (LST; ANC).

3. The Cagoule was officially known as the Comité secret d'action révolutionnaire or CSAR.

4. Vichy's anti-Semitic laws were adopted in October 1940, even before the Germans asked for them.

5. L. Darquier de Pellepoix, a virulent anti-Semite, was Xavier Vallat's successor at the CGQJ.

6. "The Phalange Africaine was the meager result of the joint agitation of collaborationist groups in Paris and Vichy, in Summer 1942. Pierre Laval was inspired by Jacques Benoist-Méchin and with the Phalange sought to give new life to military collaboration." (Henry Rousso, *La collaboration*, Paris, MA Éditions, p. 144).

7. After the 1940 armistice, the château d'Uriage, in its first incarnation, was a Pétainist officer training school.

8. Jacques Delpierré de Bayac, op. cit.

9. The 9th Brandebourg training centre was located at Paderborn in Hanover.

10. See the photographic reproduction of German files on this subject in *Maclean's*, November 15, 1951. This fact would prove to be a crucial piece of information during Bernonville's Canadian saga.

11. Darnand had been named Secretary of State for the Maintenance of Order and thus had the rank of minister.

12. See J.L. Crémieux-Brilhac, "La bataille de Glières et la guerre psychologique", *Revue d'histoire de la Deuxième Guerre mondiale*, No. 99, July 1975.

13. *Je suis partout*, April 7, 1944.

14. Ibid.

15. The Jesuit father de Montcheuil was shot along with the staff of the Vercors hospital, installed in a cave.

16. J. Delpierré de Bayac, op. cit., p. 518. The same text was published during the Bernonville affair in *The Herald*, April 27th, 1949.

17. According to Roland Haumont, Bernonville reached Germany in the automobile convoy that evacuated the SD from Paris, under the command of SS General Oberg. In Germany, he joined the 9th Brandebourg, in Paderborn. Bernonville would appear not to have been among the remnants of Vichy, that gathered around Pétain at Sigmaringen.

18. The background for this parachute operation was von Rundstedt's massive attack in the Ardennes forest at the end of 1944.

19. Bernonville later inadvertently revealed the precise location of this latter monastery, during a talk at the Université de Montréal. He claimed to have attended the ordination of 50 priests. The French secret service subsequently interpreted this information as indicating the monastery of Bétharram.

20. There are two possible versions of Jacques de Bernonville's departure for America. A memorandum of the Canadian Ministry of Immigration, dated March 29th, 1950 (DB; ANC), took note of Bernonville's deposition, according to which he boarded the passenger ship SS Ile de France in Cherbourg, Normandy on November 13th, 1946.

However, an investigation under the direction of Michel Pichard and detailed in an interview given by Roland Haumont leads one to believe Bernonville actually left for Spain. In the absence of any further information, we will stick to the latter version. According to Roland Haumont, it is very unlikely that Bernonville could have left Bétharram for Cherbourg in 1946, considering all the risks that would entail, not to mention tight controls during the boarding.

21. Interview with Roland Plourde. During his stay in Canada, Benoit-Bernonville was probably put up by other families in various towns and villages of Quebec.

CHAPTER II

Pétain's Quebec

When André Laurendeau, the editor-in-chief of *Le Devoir*, wrote his memoirs twenty years after the 1942 conscription crisis, he sought to measure the strength of Pétainist sentiment in Quebec during the war. He admitted that French Canada had greatly admired Pétain. As proof of that admiration, he called to the witness stand the nationalist leader Henri Bourassa, who had described Pétain as being "greater at Vichy than at Verdun."[1]

Laurendeau explained this attitude in part by the fact that Marshal Pétain "had done what we were prevented from doing: getting his country out of the war."[2] Besides, said the editor-in-chief, Pétain, the hero of Verdun was the best person to negotiate France's surrender. However, several decades later, it is time to look for another explanation.

Strong support for Pétainism in Quebec was clearly present among the French-Canadian élite during and after the war. This support did not come about by accident. First, Pétain's régime brought to mind another régime that was popular in Quebec. The *Estado novo* of the Portuguese dictator Salazar appealed to a significant portion of French-Canadian intellectuals, because of its alliance with the Church and its corporatist views. The French-Canadian élite, steeped in a Catholicism we would today consider fundamentalist, saw itself in the Portuguese model of a society intimately linked to the Church. Marshal Pétain never hid his admiration for the Portuguese strongman.

Second, this élite constructed a myth around French-Canadian isolationism, and also drew inspiration in France and elsewhere from the most conservative schools of thought that could possibly exist. People regularly read and subscribed to literary and political weeklies reflecting the views of the French extreme-right-wing intellectual Charles Maurras. Publications even remotely associated with left-wing causes were looked upon with suspicion. The latent and open anti-Semitism of the élites in French Canada was thereby validated. That is why, when Charles Maurras spoke of Pétain's arrival in power as a "divine surprise", his words were repeated in some Quebec circles with profound respect. The reactionary ideals of Maurras, it should be noted, had already spread to Quebec. On this side of the Atlantic, these ideals were not articulated in the same way as they were in France. The thinking of Maurras was mixed with a hodgepodge of other currents and finally adapted to the context of a French-speaking people living in North America.

Finally, the French-Canadian attitude to the French republic was conditioned by another factor: the arrival of Frenchmen fleeing what they considered to be the misdeeds of the régime in power. Priests rode high on these waves of men full of bitterness — and priests were held in high esteem in Quebec. The first contingents of priests left at the time of the French Revolution. Others followed later. Priests were still arriving in 1905, the year of the separation of Church and State in France — something the departing priests considered a violation of the privileges of the clergy in France.

Quebec was predominantly Catholic, but far from monolithic. In his book on Quebec's relationship with General de Gaulle[3], the historian Dale Thomson illustrated the cleavage between English Canadians, who tended to be supportive of de Gaulle from the beginning of the war, and French Canadians, who tended to support Pétain instead.

Within the French-Canadian population itself, there were differences of opinion over the collapse of the Third Republic and Pétain's arrival in power. The so-called nationalist newspapers and those close to the Catholic hierarchy and the clergy in general welcomed the Marshal's arrival with a great deal of hope. Meanwhile, a little liberal newspaper, Le Jour, run by Jean-Charles Harvey, published articles calling Pétain "senile". Ultimately, Thomson wrote, the whole question of 'Vichy versus de Gaulle' only interested the press and the élite. The general public remained largely indifferent.

On the whole, French-Canadian newspapers eagerly greeted Pétain as the savior of the France of old, of that France which Quebec had never stopped idolizing and idealizing. In July 1940, *La Patrie* wrote of the collapse of the Third Republic: "why mourn a régime which mistook liberty for open licentiousness?"[4]

Nationalist and Catholic newspapers in Quebec echoed the credo that was increasingly used in France to justify the reactionary character of the Vichy régime. For example, *Le Devoir* republished a poem written several years earlier by Albert Lozeau. Strangely enough, the poem anticipated the message later constructed by Vichy propaganda writers. The latter began writing in the summer of 1940 that France's defeat was a necessary ordeal if France were to be purified. Lozeau's poem read: "My friends, your France is so lovely when she bleeds!/Your France has washed her sins in her blood!/She is holy; and her dazzling throbbing heart/Is like unto the heart of Joan of Arc!"

Two days later, on June 29th, *Le Devoir* portrayed the Marshal as the most noble sort of person imaginable. The headlines over some articles published in *Le Devoir* gushed with praise: "Pétain wants to make his country French again" and "Pétain undertakes the work of national resurrection."[5] On July 13th, Omer Héroux wrote that the dark days France knew were an opportunity to throw herself "onto the path of salvation."

Moreover, the small segment of the French-Canadian population that was interested in Vichy, and in particular the lower clergy, were dazzled by a régime whose motto — Work-Family-Fatherland — prefigured the return of religious instruction into State-run schools. The newspaper *L'action catholique*, close to the hierarchy in Quebec City, applauded Pétain's reforms, although it was prevented by ecclesiastical authorities from slamming de Gaulle.

All in all, Quebec cheerfully and freely greeted Pétain's accession to power, not because Pétain represented the lesser of two evils, in the difficult circumstances created by the war, but rather because he symbolized the archetype of a régime which part of the élites longed to see established in Quebec. That is doubtless why the historian Marc Ferro rightly pointed out that Pétainism flourished in Quebec — without any Occupation.[6]

LE DEVOIR AND THE STRUGGLE AGAINST "ANTI-FRANCE"

I would like to come back for a moment to André Laurendeau's memoirs, cited above. He stated in 1962 that Quebeckers in general did not know in what conditions Vichy exercised power and they knew nothing of the fate of the French people and the Jews. According to him, French Canadians remained largely unimpressed by information then available, since they considered it to be British propaganda.

Laurendeau, having supported Pétainist ideas for a few years[7], recognized that some of his friends listened to Vichy radio broadcasts. The publisher of *Le Devoir*, Georges Pelletier, was certainly among these friends.

French Canada was a not insignificant target in the psychological war waged on short-wave radio. After the fall of France, Mason Wade related, Radio-Paris beamed a show to Quebec whose theme music was *Alouette*. The show portrayed Pétain's France in a flattering light and sought to justify Vichy's policy of collaboration. It doubtless had a small audience, since few people at the time owned a short-wave receiver.

But Georges Pelletier faithfully listened to the Marshal's speeches. Pelletier was outraged that Radio-Canada did not rebroadcast Pétain's statements over French radio, whereas Radio-Canada even distributed "the propaganda of the de Gaulle group" on recorded discs.[8]

Actually, some members of the French-Canadian élite, particularly those from the nationalist élite, not only welcomed Pétain as the regenerator of a corrupt France, but also followed with interest, and occasionally justified the way Vichy dismantled France's republican principles. In any case, they were well-informed about the changes taking place.

Frisca — we do not know who hid behind this pseudonym — wrote in *Le Devoir* on July 20, 1940:

"How far will the Pétain government go along the road of happy reforms? We do not yet know the answer. But all Catholic friends of France rejoice in the acts of renewal he has taken..."

The author then continued in the same vein:

"A country cannot be allowed, for years and even for centuries, to freely intoxicate itself with subversive doctrines, without being reduced by all sorts of calamities to moral as well as material ruin."

In his history of Jews under the Occupation, André Kaspi[9] examined the content of Vichy laws preceding the first Jewish Statute of October 1940. These earlier laws reflected the priorities of the new régime; the struggle against "anti-France", which was responsible for the defeat. Among these laws, two adopted in July 1940 opened the way. They were adopted in order to revise the conditions of naturalization; they did not exclusively target Jews, but included other members of society judged to be foreign.

The publisher of Le Devoir saw a lesson for Quebec in Vichy's change in policy. According to Pelletier, this turning-point was necessary because of the treason committed between the wars by all those who did not consider themselves French. Moreover, Pelletier urged the French Canadians to ensure that the foreign takeover of France did not also affect Quebec. On August 10, 1940, he wrote:

"Look around you, as you go about Montreal. Look at the doors of various shops, at various homes, at various small and medium-sized businesses. Look at them the way you ought to look at them. And you will see what you ought to see. Large numbers of foreigners, from all over, who are not from America except through immigration, who landed here from Germany, from Russia, from Poland, not from England or France — people just passing through, foreigners."

Pelletier did not speak openly of Jews; he let the reader guess as much, by presenting the portrait of a Quebec invaded by individuals who were neither French nor English, who were not even European and certainly not Catholic or Christian. According to him, Vichy's experience was promising, but it was not desirable, for the time being, to go as far as Vichy. After all, there were corrective measures worth taking beforehand, he said:

"The remedy is to demand that immigration be rigorously controlled, before 'storefront signs giving the complete name of the owner are put up.' Immigration in Quebec has never been controlled. These days it is controlled less than ever. Refugees are flooding in from all over (...).

"Before naturalizing anybody, a new and rigorous law should be drafted, requiring in each case serious research and inquiries."

If these immigrants knocking on Quebec's door were from the same group as those who had betrayed France, if they planned to take advantage of Quebec rather than enrich it, then action was needed. In his August 10 article, Pelletier recommended:

"Let's close the door, and keep it firmly closed. We have already had enough parasites, from whatever country, whatever their language, whatever their true ethnic origin."

Moreover, Pelletier informed his readers of developments underway at Vichy, such as the dispositions taken by Pétain to outlaw the Freemasons, or measures taken "to ensure that the dictators of French cinema, most of whom are wogs or of Jewish origin, cannot in any way return to France." [10] According to Pelletier, the protests or rather the pig-like squeals against these orders in the international press were the work of masonic sympathizers, professional anti-clericalists and avowed free-thinkers.

In October 1940, Pelletier immediately reported news of the first Jewish Statute, excluding Jews from most public offices. This time Pelletier did not openly take position. He even called the legislation anti-Semitic. However, without going so far as to support this anti-Semitism, he conceded that it was justified, on account of the expansion and arrogance of the Jewish community before the war and the presence of foreign Jews who continued doing business while Frenchmen were off at the front. For all those reasons, he concluded, Jews were not held in high esteem in Vichy France. [11]

THE FREE FRENCH HAVE A ROUGH TIME

As soon as Élisabeth de Miribel, the representative of General de Gaulle, arrived in Quebec in August 1940, she noted that French Canadians revered Pétain. She quickly realized that getting broad support for General de Gaulle was going to be an uphill struggle. In the first report she sent to London, she commented on the feelings of French Canadians: "They hope that he (Pétain) will completely remove any trace of the French Revolution and of the Republic. In their view, the government of Vichy is the only legitimate government." [12] In his biography of General de Gaulle, Jean Lacouture later wrote that the only things Quebec cared to know about France had to do with kings and priests. Élisabeth de Miribel wrote bitterly:

"French Canadians have boundless admiration for Marshal Pétain, in spite of the people surrounding him, in spite of his mistakes. They consider any news that France is being enslaved by the Nazis to be the work of English propaganda. Common folk lean toward de Gaulle. But the men in power are faithful readers of Maurras, of *Candide* and *Gringoire*, and have never tolerated France's domestic policies. Actually, they are more anti-British than anti-German. They will do everything they can to prevent Free France from being recognized in Canada, the way it already is in the United States." [14]

General de Gaulle's June 18 address to the French was not heard by many people; his August 1 address to French Canadians was received with complete indifference. The francophone spokesman of the federal government in Ottawa was relieved by that fact. "Nothing could be more dangerous," he told his colleagues, "than the birth in Quebec of a Pétain-de Gaulle controversy." [15] In any case, the federal government had difficulties trying to recognize Vichy in a way that would satisfy French Canadians, without offending their anglophone, Gaullist fellow citizens.

Despite everything, the basis for the first Gaullist committees was quickly established in Montreal and in Quebec. For those who joined the committees (mainly, although not exclusively, members of the French colony) committee work included symbolic shows of support for de Gaulle, fundraising, welcoming Free French aviators who came to Canada for training, and welcoming wounded soldiers who were being treated in Quebec.

However, some members of the French colony of Montreal played both sides. Others hindered the work of some Free French supporters. For example, Coursier, Vichy's consul in Montreal, made life hard for General de Gaulle's emissary. One day, Coursier blankly told Élisabeth de Miribel:

"Your ancestor, Marshal de Mac-Mahon, must be turning in his grave at the thought that you are working for the Judeo-Communo-Gaullists." [16]

Run-ins between Pétainists and Gaullists within the French colony, marked the establishment of the first committees. The historian
Marcel Trudel had a professor of French literature at Laval University,
Auguste Viatte, who was of Swiss origin and a Gaullist. The latter was
ostracized by one of his French colleagues who was totally committed
to Pétain.

By openly supporting de Gaulle, Viatte was clearly going against
French-Canadian public opinion. Even so, that did not prevent him from
setting up a Free French committee in Quebec along with Marthe
Simard, an important figure in the Free French movement. According
to Robert Cornevin, this initiative, combined with others of the same
kind, eventually bore fruit and succeeded in creating something of a
Gaullist atmosphere in Quebec.[17] But Montreal would remain a prob-
lem for the Gaullists, since Vichy supporters deployed the greater part
of their forces there.

When Marthe Simard came to Quebec, she advised Élisabeth de
Miribel not to attack Pétain directly. During a conference at Laval
University, de Gaulle's representative did what she could to follow this
advice, although it took a lot of self-control:

"A first question is put to me point-blank: 'What do you think of
Marshal Pétain's reforms?' I keep my cool and say only that 'As
long as France is divided up in three zones, the forbidden zone, the
occupied zone and the supposedly free zone, domestic reforms do
not interest me.' The very young French Canadian addressing me
replies placidly: 'As for us, we have been occupied for two hundred
years by the English, and reforms interest us a lot!' I preferred not
to reply."[18]

In March 1941, the arrival of de Gaulle's prestigious emissary,
Commander Georges Thierry d'Argenlieu[19], did not melt the Pétainist
ice any better. De Gaulle wisely sent this naval officer and member of
a French religious community to the very Catholic province of Quebec.
D'Argenlieu had flirted at first with Pétainism before joining de Gaulle.
He was received with all honors by Cardinal Rodrigue Villeneuve, and
was at the centre of controversy during his stay. The Benedictine Dom
Albert Jamet, who was of French origin and had left France several
years previously, ripped into him in the pages of *Le Devoir*.

But the most devastating attack came from a new review published
in Quebec by a group of unconditional Pétainists. *La Droite*, founded

at the beginning of 1941, was established as a corporatist, nationalist, Catholic and Pétainist review designed to educate the common people. Father Simon Arsenault, a professor of political economy, built up a young team of contributors that included Jacques Sauriol and Doris Lussier.

In the April issue (the fourth), featuring a portrait of Marshal Pétain on the cover, Thierry d'Argenlieu the emissary was lambasted. According to the authors of the article, he was a mere sailor, or even a traveling salesman doing treacherous work on behalf of a rebellious general, who was the real target of the article.

In fact, this is a crucial text for the understanding of Quebec Pétainism. The author, Doris Lussier, wrote:

"It was not enough for this disloyal, stubborn and headstrong general to flee his country at the supreme moment, when he was called upon to do his last duty, and dress the wounds of the Nation. No, this individual had to undertake in a foreign country an insidious campaign to discredit the world over, and in all French circles of the Universe, the only man in France who could find in his old soldier's heart the love and courage he needed to face the deserters and tell them 'Whatever happens, I shall not abandon the soil of the Nation. I make an offering of my person to France, in order to lessen her suffering.'

"We have made our choice between de Gaulle, the cowardly fugitive who, in the hour of danger, simply cleared off, and Pétain, who symbolizes the purest and most intelligent patriotism that can be imagined..." [20]

Lussier felt that putting de Gaulle on trial would be too easy; it would involve too much talking. According to Lussier, de Gaulle certainly did not represent the "real France". After the death of the unmourned Third Republic, the "real France" was flourishing once again, thanks to another soldier who was stationed in Vichy.

"(...) The 'Real France', the France of St. Louis and Joan of Arc, of corporations and Crusades, has cast its filthy republican and anticlerical and secular clothing into the dirty-laundry bin, in order to find once more, under the guidance of the glorious Marshal, that traditional and Christian and radiant face it used to have, before the revolutionary and obscurantist philosophers of 1789 covered it, smeared and disfigured it." [21]

For Doris Lussier, the old individualist world was dying and a corporatist rebirth reminiscent of the Middle Ages was coming about. For 150 years, the world had been drinking from the enchanting but poisoned chalice of Liberty; as a result, the world knew only chaos, bloody revolutions and wars.

"Europe and the world are dying because of Liberty wrongly-conceived; let them free themselves from the clutches of the old man. And let us ready ourselves to see Europe and the world rise again in the light of Authority, of that authority which is superior to and far-removed from individualist liberalism and animal totalitarianism alike.

"Following the examples of Salazar's Portugal, of Franco's Spain and of France, of the dear, sweet France of Pétain, all humanity will be born once again in the radiant sun of justice and charity, under the saintly crown of peace, glory and immortality." [22]

But the review was closed abruptly — perhaps because of the veiled threats made by Father Arsenault, when he asked whether defeating Vichy was an Allied war aim. He warned right away: "For us, Pétain is the new France, namely the France which has been purged of her parasites and her vices (...).French Canadians had this same France for a mother and they are proud to say today they are her son...." [23] According to Arsenault, French Canadians had no thought of dissociating themselves from the war, unless the war were waged against Vichy France, which they rightfully supported.

A few days later, the Royal Canadian Mounted Police, acting on federal orders, seized the review and shut it down forever. A year later, *L'Union*, a nationalist newspaper in Montreal, inspired by Paul Gouin, René Chaloult and Philippe Hamel, adopted the Pétainist motto Work-Family-Fatherland. The newspaper campaigned against conscription and sought to unmask a secret coalition of Jews against French Canadians.

As a result, during the greater part of the war, the Free French did not get good press in Quebec. They were occasionally referred to with derision as "Free French" in English (rather than "Français libres", to underline their subservience to Winston Churchill's England. In July

1942, an opinion poll revealed that 75 % of Quebec inhabitants continued to approve of Pétain's policies.[24] Four months later, Roger Duhamel slammed the Gaullists in an article in *Le Devoir*. The author vilified those Gaullists established in America and whose names all too frequently sounded Jewish.[25]

During this period, the Société St. Jean Baptiste also refused to allow a group of Free French supporters to take part in its June 24 parade. The nationalist organization claimed it took this decision because the French colony of Montreal did not unanimously support de Gaulle.[26]

In carefully studying the sequence of events, one sees that the anti-English reflex did not initially play a role in French-Canadian support for Pétain. Anti-English sentiment was an essential part of conservative nationalism at the time, but ended up playing another role: it served as a weapon in attempts to justify the slander campaign waged from the very beginning against de Gaulle. Indeed, de Gaulle was rightly seen as a London-based adversary, waging a bitter struggle against the Marshal and the National Revolution.

If we indulged for a moment in political fiction, we could imagine the Communist Maurice Thorez in Pétain's place in Summer 1940. In that case, French Canadians would not have supported the new régime, and the campaign against de Gaulle in Quebec would probably never have taken place.

Anti-English sentiment cropped up again in 1942, during the conscription crisis. There were some similarities between the anti-English sentiment used to justify hostility to de Gaulle and the anti-English sentiment used to bolster opposition to the mobilization of troops, but it is important to draw a distinction between the two sentiments.

Other groups of the French-Canadian élite embraced the Gaullists with enthusiasm. Among them were to be found Edmond Turcotte, the publisher of the liberal newspaper *Le Canada*, Jean-Charles Harvey, René Garneau and Jean-Louis Gagnon. A brilliant journalist in Montreal, Louis Francoeur, analyzed news from the front over the radio. He did so on a daily basis and with considerable tact; little by little, he helped bring many French Canadians over to General de Gaulle's side. The new federal justice minister, Louis St. Laurent, and others such as Cardinal Villeneuve, also exerted influence in favor of the Allies. Villeneuve, for example, reprimanded the editorial team at *La Droite*, and there is no doubt that the police seizure of the review threw Pétainist intellectuals into a panic.

In short, a big change was taking place. The change can be said to have started in 1942, after the April referendum on conscription, in which French Canadians and English Canadians divided into two distinctive blocs: one against mandatory mobilization and the other for it. But this change should be qualified and quantified. The nationalist and Catholic press now fully supported the war aims of the Allies, and consequently Free France, and paid close attention to theatres of war where French-Canadian soldiers were active. Even so, the nationalist and Catholic press accepted de Gaulle under duress rather than of its own free will. In secret, its heart was still with Pétain. Quebec Pétainism was just asleep, temporarily laid on the shelf.

On February 3, 1943, three months after the Germans occupied the whole territory of France, a headline in *Le Devoir* read, "Marshal Pétain remains the mystical symbol of his Nation." The thesis of de Gaulle the sword and Pétain the shield firmly took root. At a time when support for Pétain had already begun to weaken in France, the breach in the Pétain fortress of Quebec had hardly been opened.

LIKE THE MOSCOW SHOW-TRIALS

The fact that large crowds welcomed General de Gaulle during his Quebec visit in July 1944 definitely helped create support for him. However, as Jean Lacouture noted, the warmth of that reception did not bring de Gaulle back to Quebec the following year, although he was nearby in Ottawa.

Two months after the visit and three weeks before the liberation of Paris, the newspaper *Le Bloc*, published by the Bloc Populaire Canadien, regretted that de Gaulle had uttered such hurtful words about Pétain. The newspaper, which had already denounced the arrival in Canada of "yids of fighting age", established a distinction between Laval, Darnand and others like them, "who doubtless developed their collaborationist sentiments to the hilt" — and an old man, the Marshal, whom it was hard to condemn.[27]

In January 1945, at the time of the trial of the writer Robert Brasillach, the campaign led by François Mauriac and others to obtain a pardon was widely discussed in Quebec. The conviction of the former editor-in-chief of *Je suis partout* and the symbol of intellectual collaboration created a stir among some French-Canadian leaders.

Once intellectuals and parliamentarians like André Laurendeau refused to get involved in the affair, organizers turned to nationalist associations. Ultimately, the Société St. Jean Baptiste de Montréal and the Société nationale des Canadiens français delivered a resolution to France's ambassador in Ottawa against inflicting the death penalty on intellectuals accused of collaboration. Immediately afterward, another more Gaullist group made up of writers and journalists publicly expressed their disagreement with the resolution. The position taken by Jean-Charles Harvey, Jean-Louis Gagnon, Guy Jasmin and Roger Lemelin confirmed the division that would continue into the postwar period between supporters of de Gaulle and of Pétain.

The trial of Henri-Philippe Pétain in July 1945 opened an important rift between Quebec and the France of de Gaulle. That same year in Montreal, the philosophy professor Louis Rougier published an account of wartime events in France strengthening the thesis that the Marshal had played a double game.

The publisher of the *Bloc*, Léopold Richer, took up this version of the facts and came out in defense of Pétain. "France resisted in the free zone and the colonies. Pétain, Weygand and Darlan resisted." [28] In order to accept this truth, he said, it was necessary not to be blinded by political passions.

Pétain's conviction created a division in the French-Canadian press. *Le Jour* and *Le Canada* did not make much of a fuss over it, while the clerico-nationalist press, led by *L'Action catholique*, saw an act of masonic vengence, or, put another way, a repetition of the "assassination of Louis XVI." [29]

On August 15, 1945 Paul Sauriol wrote in *Le Devoir* that the trial had "dealt a formidable blow to France's prestige in the world." Sauriol compared the conviction to the Moscow show trials. Sauriol was one of the first people in Quebec to denounce the revolutionary purges that had been raging since the Liberation. He considered the Marshal's trial as one of the darkest episodes in France's history.

For his part, the historian Robert Rumilly slammed Pétain adversaries in the ferociously antisocialist newspaper *Vers demain*: "From Jewry to Freemasonry by way of the Intelligence Service, all the forces raised against Franco are also the mortal enemies of French Canada. Those among us who help these forces are insane or treacherous." [30]

Rumilly was considering the possibility of writing Pétain's biography, in order to rehabilitate him in Canada. During the Summer of 1946, one of his good friends from Quebec City, Maurice Vincent, made a pilgrimage to Ile d'Yeu where Pétain was interned, and entered into contact with the Marshal's wife as well as his lawyer, Jacques Isorni. The latter said he was ready to provide the historian from Canada with any documentation needed for his work. Rumilly never followed through with his idea. However, during the next few months, he would discover other ways of taking direct action. Ultimately, his new activities converged toward the same objectives.

FOOTNOTES

1. André Laurendeau, *La crise de la conscription, 1942*, Montreal, Les Éditions du Jour, 1962, p. 115.

2. Ibid.

3. Dale C. Thomson, *De Gaulle et le Québec*, St. Laurent, Éditions du Trécarré, 1990, chap. 3.

4. Cited by Mason Wade in *The French Canadians from 1760 to 1967*.

5. *Le Devoir*, July 12, 1940.

6. Marc Ferro, Pétain, Paris, Fayard, 1987, p. 687.

7. Interview with André Malavoy, a Resistance member from the beginning of the Occupation, who settled in Montreal in 1951. André Malavoy knew André Laurendeau well. After taking part in the radio show *Pays et merveilles*, hosted by Laurendeau, Malavoy was asked to write his war memoirs. The book, entitled *La mort attendra*, was published by the Éditions de l'Homme in Montreal in 1961. Malavoy believes moreover that he helped "liquidate" Laurendeau's last Pétainist convictions starting in the early 1950s. (It should be noted that Quebec Pétainism was expressed generally in terms of "sympathy" for the Marshal himself, and by extension for certain ideas defended by his régime.) During a conference on André Laurendeau, André Malavoy said that "Vichy France had considerable prestige in the eyes of Quebeckers. Laurendeau himself hesitated to reject it outright, but he conceded that he could have only an abstract and therefore incomplete idea of what Vichy really was, while my passionate condemnation was backed up by everything I had suffered in body and blood. He went so far as to thank me for helping him open his eyes on the subject. Yes, he was enriched by others just as he in turn enriched others." Robert Comeau and Lucille Beaudry (editors), *André Laurendeau, un intellectuel d'ici*, Presses de l'Université du Québec, 1990, p. 16.

8. Georges Pelletier in *Le Devoir*, August 14, 1940.

9. André Kaspi, *Les Juifs pendant l'Occupation*, Paris, Seuil, 1991.

10. Georges Pelletier, in *Le Devoir*, August 15, 1940.

11. Ibid., October 18, 1940.

12. Dale C. Thompson, op cit., p. 42.

13. Jean Lacouture, *De Gaulle*, vol. 3: *Le souverain*, Paris, Seuil, 1986, p. 510.

14. Élisabeth de Miribel, *La liberté souffre violence*, Paris, Plon, 1981, p. 51.

15. Dale C. Thompson, op. cit., p. 41.

16. Élisabeth de Miribel, op. cit., p. 53.

17. According to Cornevin, the attitude of Viatte, Simard and their group contributed to "creating a Gaullist atmosphere in Quebec City, unlike the atmosphere in Montreal and in French Canada as a whole." Robert Cornevin, "Auguste Viatte, maître et pionnier des littératures de langue française", *Mélanges Auguste Viatte*, Paris, Académie sciences d'outre-mer, 1981, p. 11.

18. Élisabeth de Miribel, op. cit., p. 55.

19. Captain Thierry d'Argenlieu was Carmelite provincial, under the name of Father Louis de la Trinité.

20. Doris Lussier, in *La Droite*, Quebec, vol. 1, No. 4, April 15, 1941, pp. 19-20.

21. Ibid.

22. Ibid.

23. Father Simon Arsenault, ibid., p. 7. (In her memoirs published in 1981, Élisabeth de Miribel recalled the "repulsive articles" about the Gaullists published in *La Droite*. See Élisabeth de Miribel, op. cit., p. 79, and Conrad Black, *Duplessis*, Toronto, McClelland & Stewart, 1977.

24. Dale C. Thomson, op. cit., p. 80.

25. Roger Duhamel in *Le Devoir*, November 28, 1942.

26. Robert Rumilly, *Histoire de la Société Saint Jean Baptiste de Montréal*, Montreal, L'Aurore, p. 519.

27. *Le Bloc*, September 9, 1944.

28. Ibid., July 4, 1945.

29. Jean Lacouture, op. cit. p. 510.

30. *Vers demain*, August 15, 1945.

CHAPTER III

The fugitives

R obert Rumilly was the real kingpin of the semi-clandestine organization that helped some French fugitives start a new life in Canada, beginning in Spring 1947. Most of these fugitives were veterans of the Milice, supporters of the Milice, or ardent supporters of Vichy, who arrived in Quebec starting in Summer 1946.[1] They fled the purges in France where they knew they faced convictions, and quickly got into contact with Rumilly.

Joseph Rudel-Tessier, one of his good friends, wrote one day that Rumilly embodied the very ideal of the émigré having fled the persecutions of the French Revolution, along with the nobility. Calling him "the last of the émigrés" summed up his convictions, although other people did eventually follow in his footsteps.

Robert Rumilly was born in 1897 in Fort-de-France, Martinique — the same year as Jacques de Bernonville, also known as Jacques Benoit. With his father, an officer in the colonial army, he then moved on to Indochina. Rumilly became an orphan at an early age and studied in Paris. During the First World War, he enlisted in the army.

After that disastrous war ended, Rumilly joined the Action française. Along with his fellow students, members like him of the Royalist combat group "les Camelots du Roi", he marched in step in the streets of Paris. Rumilly became a disciple of Charles Maurras and got to know the future leaders of the extreme-right movement. He also made the acquaintance of Count Jacques de Bernonville.

In 1928, when he was 30 years old, Rumilly, now a shopkeeper, left France for Quebec, where he was hired by a company ironically named "Scandale". Rumilly fell in love with French Canada at first sight. He quickly made the adjustment to the Catholic French-speaking people, who had, in his view, just the right dose of modernity. The former Camelot du Roi projected onto this society his dreams of the long-lost France of old.

Rumilly worked day and night, and began to publish historical biographies. Then, he undertook his lifework, a series of books recounting the history of the province of Quebec since Confederation in 1867. To make the job easier, he accepted various jobs as a federal civil servant in Ottawa, in order to be closer to the archives which contained a treasure of first-hand accounts. Rumilly patiently opened up an immense historical field. He never took holidays. He worked seven days a week, 12 hours a day, and eventually became a respected historian. In 1944, he was appointed to the newly-created Académie canadienne-française.

Rumilly was a tall, austere gentleman with slit eyes hidden by thick spectacles. His deep voice and his manner gave him a certain aristocratic air. He was generous with his friends and even downright funny. In the presence of his adversaries, however, he became a cold and intransigent machine.

Rumilly was a historian but also a polemicist. He had opinions about everything. During World War Two, he almost joined his friend Camillien Houde in an internment camp because of his ferocious opposition to conscription. He was a Royalist and Pétainist during the war, and also a fervent anti-Freemason, anti-Communist and anti-Semite. Rumilly's friend Rudel-Tessier wrote down some remarks Rumilly made after 1945 about the Holocaust. Rumilly merely scolded Hitler, the dictator, for having only booted the Jews out of Germany.[2]

When it came to the nationalist historian abbé Lionel Groulx, Rumilly had relations that were courteous but also marked by a certain professional rivalry. Rumilly played the role of intellectual leader of the right-wing movement in Quebec, but in a much less discreet fashion than the abbé and at a different level. In 1947, he would serve as an inspiration for those Quebeckers who would support French Catholics who had remained loyal to the ideal of the Marshal. He felt that these victims of the purges were the most likely people to get along with French Canadians.

"THE PURE MUST HELP ONE ANOTHER"

In Spring 1947, Jacques Benoit was transferred by his company in St. Pacôme to Montreal, where he was to take care of lumber sales abroad. Unfortunately, several weeks later, he lost his job. Rumilly then intervened, to help him find work elsewhere. The historian felt a great deal of sympathy for this family in hiding, and became the godfather of one of Benoit's daughters, Chantal. He gave his 18-year-old god-daughter financial help, which she greatly appreciated, and used to pay tuition fees at university.

Rumilly showed the same concern for his former companion in the Action française. While Benoit looked for a new job, Rumilly suggested to Jean Bonnel, a businessman of French origin and a die-hard Pétainist, that they club together to raise a little cash among like-minded friends. This cash could help pay the family's rent, he said.

Rumilly did the rounds of businessmen he knew well in search of a job for Benoit. He quickly realized that he had to move beyond the circle of active Pétainists. After visiting the "purest of the pure", Rumilly advised Benoit to adopt a new strategy and "to talk the language of business, rather than of feelings."[3]

Jean Bonnel, who made a point of protecting veterans of the Milice and all kinds of Vichy supporters in Quebec, guided Benoit in his search for a job. Bonnel explained to Rumilly: "the pure must help one another."[4]

While waiting to find something more attractive, Jacques Benoit got jobs as a mechanic, a truck oiler and a car washer, before finally landing a job in a milk products company. During this period, the Benoit family regularly traveled to Quebec to visit their good friend, Doctor Georges Montel, and his family. Montel was in Annecy during the Occupation. He was named assistant mayor by the Vichy government, and fled before the end of the war, since he was being pursued by the Resistance. After many ups and downs, including a stay in Switzerland, he ended up in Quebec at Laval University. Sharing the secrets of these families was a little close-knit community, drawn together by a common devotion to the person of Pétain.

At the end of Fall 1947, Benoit began working for the Compagnie franco-canadienne de produits laitiers (the Franco-Canadian Dairy Products Company), thanks to the help of a certain Jacques Fichet, a businessman of French origin who had already been in Canada for 30 years. Like Bonnel, Fichet had strongly pro-Vichy convictions.

Benoit's new job took him to Granby. That is where, in mid-December 1947, he met an individual he would have preferred never to have known, named Jokelson. Jokelson and Bernonville had known each other in the early 1930s in Paris. Both had worked on the same storey of the same building, but for two different companies: Bernonville, for the SAGA shipping company (Société anonyme de gérance et d'armement) and Jokelson for the Dreyfus company, specialists in maritime transportation. The two men naturally ran into each other on occasion. Due to circumstances, they quickly lost sight of one another, and did not meet again during the war.

Jokelson was a French citizen of Jewish origin. His grandparents had emigrated from Denmark. During the war, he worked in the Resistance for the intelligence service. His wife was arrested by the Gestapo and died in a prison camp. When the Germans surrounded the building he was in, he just barely managed to escape, by slipping out of a window.

After the war, Jokelson started working once again for Dreyfus and was sent to Canada to organize shipments of foodstuffs to postwar France. Since dairy products were on the list of supplies needed in France, Jokelson went to Granby, where he suddenly ran into Bernonville. The veteran of the Resistance greeted Bernonville by his real name, since that was the only name he knew. Bernonville was taken aback and stuttered that he was now known as Jacques Benoit.

Needless to say, Bernonville's reaction gave Jokelson pause. He found the story suspicious, and his familiarity with the Intelligence Service helped him uncover more information. He got in touch with friends from the Resistance who had remained in France and also with retired Colonel Michel Pichard, now a resident of Montreal.[5] During the war, Pichard had used various code-names, such as Pic, Picolo and Gauss; he had played an important role in the Resistance, serving for example as national coordinator of the Bloc des Opérations Aériennes (BOA). Working completely underground, he had many people under his command organizing Allied parachute drops of supplies.

Meanwhile, Bernonville sensed that he had been compromised by Jokelson and therefore decided to take matters into his own hands. In mid-January 1948, he and his family reported to an immigration officer in Montreal. Bernonville revealed his true identity and asked that he and his family be admitted as Canadian citizens. They were then sent before a council that would look into their request. The immigration procedure got underway, and included an interview with the applicants and a medical exam. That would be followed up by a decision to accept or reject their request, and ultimately a deportation order if necessary.

Things did not look promising for Bernonville. But they looked even worse for one of his compatriots and friends, Dr. Montel. Indeed, Montel's Quebec hosts would soon wage a furious battle in the hopes of keeping him in Canada.

A SEMINARY DESIGNATED AS A SANCTUARY

In February 1948, Dr. Georges Montel, on the staff of Laval University in Quebec City, received an expulsion order from Canadian authorities. Over the last few months, Montel had been pushing his request to become a Canadian citizen, with the help of Senator Jean-Marie Dessureault. As a result, he had to reveal his real identity and admit that he had illegally entered Canada using false papers. The measures taken by the senator were worse than disappointing; they were simply catastrophic. While Montel had hoped to obtain a permanent visa, he had received an expulsion order instead. Mgr. Ferdinand Vandry, the rector of Laval University, had been waiting for Montel's application to be approved before offering him a full-time position as a faculty member of the university. The latest events had called everything into question.

The ecclesiastical authorities in Quebec City got together and launched a campaign to save Montel. They took pains to ensure that the campaign made no waves, and that Montel was not overtly subject to favoritism. Only the most discreet and prudent measures were to be taken. Mgr. Vandry and the archbishop of Quebec, Mgr. Maurice Roy, headed the pressure group. At this point, what they knew about Montel's past included his appointment by the Vichy government to the prefect's office in Annecy, his past as a well-known anti-Communist, his run-ins with the Resistance and finally his escape to Canada.[6]

The Quebec bishops intended to force federal civil servants to reverse their decision, by appealing directly to political authorities in Ottawa. The bishops counted on the guidance of the independent MP Frédéric Dorion and Senator Jean-Marie Dessureault. Rumilly waited for the time being, but kept abreast of the affair along with two friends in Quebec City: the provincial deputy René Chaloult and the dentist

Philippe Hamel. Mgr. Vandry kept the historian well-informed, reassured him and let him know that "a carefully-orchestrated action plan is being executed at the moment on several fronts."[7] The archbishop of Quebec, Mgr. Maurice Roy, echoed those sentiments: "you can rest assured," he said, "that I will take every possible measure to make sure that Dr. Montel can settle in Canada."[8]

Meanwhile, Mgr. Vandry got in touch with Cardinal Gerlier in France, to get him to bring pressure to bear on the government of Georges Bidault. People in Quebec City suspected that the French government wanted to make life difficult for Montel. Vandry said to Chaloult that he would be willing to renounce his Légion d'honneur decoration if the situation got any worse. "I would prefer to keep my honour than the Légion d'honneur," he said.[9]

In their campaign on behalf of Montel, the two ecclesiastics concentrated their efforts on the French-Canadian spokesman in the Ottawa government, the former Quebec City lawyer Louis St. Laurent. But murmurs and hints simply weren't getting the message across, and the two did not succeed in convincing St. Laurent of the imperative of acting.

Rumilly and his friends started to lose patience, especially since Dr. Montel only had a few months left before his expulsion order would come into effect. Rumilly was a civil servant in Ottawa, and decided to personally take in hand the pressure campaign, by seeking the support of other bishops. He shared his concerns with an openly Pétainist ecclesiastic, the Benedictine Dom Albert Jamet. Rumilly asked him to do everything possible to get the top ecclesiastical authorities in the land to lobby St. Laurent directly. Dom Jamet, who had lambasted General de Gaulle's envoy in 1941, no longer had the same amount of energy (he was to die a few months later), but offered his services nonetheless. "I believe neither in the generosity not in the sincerity of St. Laurent," the Benedictine wrote to Rumilly. "He didn't wait to become leader of the government before betraying all the causes of French Canadians." [10]

Dom Jamet assessed those ecclesiastical forces in Quebec ready to take part in the campaign to help Montel. According to his assessment, some bishops were likely to make only moderate commitments to avoid compromising themselves. But Dom Jamet did not give up easily: "I believe less in the number of interventions than in their quality," he told Rumilly.[11] The Benedictine was also hopeful about the Université de Montréal. The dean of the Faculty of Arts, Canon

Sideleau, was a former classmate of St. Laurent's. According to Dom Jamet, Sideleau would be able to counter the "tissue of lies" about Montel transmitted by the French authorities.

Jean Houpert, an employee of the Université de Montréal and a man who sympathized with Montel's cause from the very beginning, got Sideleau to promise he would intervene. Even better, he got a commitment from the rector of the Université de Montréal, Mgr. Olivier Maurault. In the days that followed, Canon Sideleau did indeed contact St. Laurent. The minister told him that he could not come to a decision until Canada's ambassador in Paris, Georges Vanier, had sent him a full report on Dr. Montel's real activities during the Occupation.

Time was running out and the expulsion order was still in effect. Mgr. Vandry was determined to keep Montel at Laval University at any price. As a result, in Spring 1948 he dreamed up a new strategy: planning Montel's escape to the Quebec Seminary in the event that the agents of the Immigration department sought to deport him by fair means or foul. "We shall see," he said to Montel, "whether they dare come to get you under my roof." [12] In the same breath, he warned Georges Bideault in Paris and the French embassy in Ottawa that there would be an explosive scandal if France continued to slander Montel.

The idea of transforming the Quebec Seminary into a sanctuary never materialized. On May 6, while Rumilly was attending a recital by Maurice Chevalier in Ottawa, he happened to meet a French-Canadian minister in the federal cabinet. Rumilly spoke of his great disappointment considering that French-language deputies had done so little to help. To his astonishment the minister offered an encouraging response.

Listening to the words of the minister Bertrand, Rumilly understood that the bishops had not been sufficiently energetic in their efforts on behalf of Montel. Moreover, people in Ottawa seemed to want the archbishop and the rector to get more involved. In other words, if the archbishop and rector were willing to vouch for Montel, that would be welcomed by Ottawa and could serve as a reply to Paris. France had not formally requested Montel's extradition, but was now aware that Montel was in Canada.

"Let them vouch for him, and that will justify our decision," said the minister. "We are not going to set the Quebec clergy against us. If Mgr. Vandry — and even better Mgr. Roy — want to let St. Laurent or me know, in writing or over the telephone, that they insist on Montel's getting a visa, we will deliver. I promise you I will await their say-so, and the expulsion order will not be executed in the meantime." [13]

The minister kept his promise and the next day the suspension of the order was confirmed. But Montel's fate still hadn't been determined. The temporary suspension only meant the timetable had changed. His friends asked what they should do. The work undertaken so far and the results obtained seemed pretty doubtful. Besides, people said, others would probably soon follow in Montel's footsteps.

LIKE WANDERING JEWS

While the plan to offer Montel asylum in the Quebec Seminary was being developed, some people, such as the autonomist deputy René Chaloult, already understood that there was a lesson to be learned. Chaloult, an independent representative in the provincial legislature for the Quebec City region, was a longtime proponent of the nationalist thinking of abbé Groulx. He had closely followed the Montel affair as it unfolded, and had believed since the previous Spring that it was necessary to alert the press and intervene in the House of Commons in Ottawa and the Legislature in Quebec City. Mgr. Vandry held him back. Dr. Montel agreed with his rector, and believed that a public campaign in his favour could do him more harm than good.

Anticipating that a change in tactics was on the way, Rumilly and his friends drew up a list of French citizens having fled to Canada to escape the purges. Besides Jacques de Bernonville and Georges Montel, the presence of four other fugitives in Montreal was established, namely Julien Labedan, Jean Louis Huc, André Boussat and Michel Seigneur.

Rumilly leaned more and more towards mobilizing public opinion in their favor. As a result, he got in contact with some of the fugitives in order to gather all the information that could be mustered in their defence when the timing was right. In Spring 1948, he became friendly with Julien Labedan, who was awaiting the outcome of the government investigation to determine whether he could remain in Canada. Labedan confided to Rumilly that "I definitely do not have the courage to leave this country (...) and like a wandering Jew try to settle in other countries as unwilling as this one to welcome the fugitives of Europe." [14]

Julien Labedan presented himself as an outlaw who had "tried to stop the odious advance of Communism" during the Occupation.[15] As a member of the Milice, he had served in operations against the

Resistance, but towards the end of the war he joined the French forces of General Leclerc. Then, after being condemned to death in absentia in January 1945, he went into hiding in Brittany. Concealing his true identity, he finally managed to get out of France with forged papers and the help of a religious community. He arrived in Canada on July 30, 1946.

The story of Jean Louis Huc resembled that of Labedan. A former member of the Milice, he was sentenced at the end of the war to five years in prison. Huc arrived in Sorel on June 14, 1946, under the pseudonym of Jean Henry, with the title of chargé de mission for the French ministry of the Merchant Marine. After that, Gustave Piché, a senior civil servant in the Quebec department of Lands and Forests introduced him to Senator Dessureault in order to help him with his request for Canadian citizenship.

In June 1948, Julien Labedan and Jean Louis Huc were facing an expulsion order. Rumilly was upset, and realized that the Dessureault connection was of little use. Worse still, on July 2, his friend and the father of his god-daughter, Jacques de Bernonville, informed him that if nothing was done, he would be deported from Canada in exactly two months. The Bernonville family had just 60 days to get out of the country.

THE ARREST OF THE BERNONVILLE FAMILY

As soon as he learned the news, Rumilly took vigorous new measures in Ottawa. He wanted to regularize the status of the French fugitives he knew about. Rumilly was so annoyed by the apathy shown by French-Canadian ministers towards the fugitives that he decided to leave the federal civil service himself. On July 14, he presented his resignation in order to be "free to say, to write and if need be to *yell* what (he) thinks." [16]

Now that Rumilly was free to act, he threw himself into the political fray and first of all into the election campaign then under way in Quebec. During Summer 1948, he became a pamphleteer for the Union Nationale of Maurice Duplessis, the party seeking to conserve power in Quebec. On July 28, Duplessis won the election.

Before leaving Ottawa, Rumilly had warned federal ministers that they would have "a big scandal" on their hands if they didn't do as he said. He now calculated every possible means of intervening.

Moreover, he kept his friend Camillien Houde, the mayor of Montreal, abreast of the situation. Rumilly had a powerful intellectual influence on the mayor. After spending four years in an internment camp, Houde had tried to keep well away from this kind of cause. During the 1945 Brasillach trial, for example, he had refused to join forces with Rumilly in order to defend the accused and others implicated in the trial.

But Houde was a populist orator, and naturally kept in touch with Rumilly. Along with Rumilly, Houde even considered for awhile the possibility of creating a new nationalist party devoted to defending the interests of French Canadians on the federal scene. In Spring 1948, Houde heard about Dr. Montel's problems, and spoke of quickly launching a campaign in his defense, along with Premier Duplessis. Mgr. Vandry's instructions held him back.

Then suddenly came a bombshell. On Thursday, September 2, on the day before Labor Day, Rumilly broke the unbelievable news to Houde that Jacques de Bernonville and his family had been arrested that very morning and were currently detained in the offices of the Immigration department on rue St. Antoine in Montreal. According to Immigration authorities, they would be deported by the following Monday.

Now it was essential that someone with the political clout of Camillien Houde enter the scene. Rumilly pleaded with him to intervene.

"You can mobilize public opinion," Rumilly told him.

"Listen," replied Houde, "I am thunderstruck by this news. I am going to cancel my appointments, leave my office and go home. Call me back in an hour."

A few minutes later, Houde had made up his mind.

"Once again, I am going to be at the centre of a storm. But it's my duty, I will do it, I will appeal to public opinion." [17]

FOOTNOTES

1. Vichy and the Collaboration are two subjects that should be treated with great caution. One should also resist the temptation to lump together the following terms: crimes against humanity, war crimes, collaboration, collaborationism and the Vichy ideology. The present work refers more generally to "collaborators" and "presumed collaborators", especially since these were the words used at the time, particularly by the English-language press.

2. Notes for a biography of Robert Rumilly by Joseph Rudel-Tessier (RR; ANQ; 10).

3. Letter from Robert Rumilly to Jacques Benoit (Bernonville), May 20, 1947 (RR; ANQ; 14).

4. Letter from Jean Bonnel to Robert Rumilly, May 23, 1947 (RR; ANQ; 14).

5. See on this subject Henri Noguères, *Histoire de la Résistance en France*, Paris, Laffont, 1972, vol. 3, p. 509.

6. Undated notes for the defence of Georges Montel (RR; ANQ; 14).

7. Letter from Mgr. Ferdinand Vandry to Robert Rumilly, February 25, 1948 (RR; ANQ; 14).

8. Letter from Mgr. Maurice Roy to Robert Rumilly, February 28, 1948 (RR; ANQ; 14).

9. Letter from René Chaloult to Robert Rumilly, February 27, 1948 (RR; ANQ; 14).

10. Letter from Dom Albert Jamet to Robert Rumilly, February 28, 1948 (RR; ANQ; 14).

11. Ibid.

12. Letter from René Chaloult to Robert Rumilly, April 9, 1948 (RR; ANQ; 12)

13. Letter from Robert Rumilly to René Chaloult, May 7, 1948 (RR; ANQ; 14).

14. Letter from Julien Labedan to Robert Rumilly, Spring 1948 (RR; ANQ; 14).

15. Ibid.

16. Letter from Robert Rumilly to Ernest Bertrand, July 14, 1948 (RR; ANQ; 14).

17. Transcript of a CKAC radio talk given by Robert Rumilly, Spring 1951 (RR; ANQ; 14).

CHAPTER IV

A provincial affair

A t the outset of the affair, the Canadian public as a whole knew nothing about Jacques de Bernonville's true past. Even among the small circle of pro-Vichy Quebeckers inspired by Robert Rumilly, few people had entirely accurate information about him. In any case, that wasn't really so important. Bernonville told them he was loyal to Marshal Pétain, and that was enough. His precise role in the Collaboration with the Nazis was of secondary importance. They were willing to see his Collaboration as a sort of extension of the Marshal's will, whatever real consequences that might have had. And so it was that Camillien Houde presided over the kick-off on September 3, 1948.

On that day, the mayor of Montreal contacted the British United Press agency and publicized the plans of federal bureaucrats to deport Count Jacques Dugé de Bernonville within a few days. The following day, newspapers and radio alike spoke of little else. In its September 4 edition, the Montreal daily newspaper *La Presse* splashed an eight-column-wide headline over its front page: "Sensational arrest. Vichy man under death sentence is arrested in Montreal." The readers learned from the article what position their mayor intended to adopt in this affair. The work of disinformation had begun.

The article gave a foretaste of the battle to come. "Which is to say," Houde told the journalists, "that a man will be sacrificed for political reasons, whereas his only fault was probably to have executed the orders he received and which were not to the taste of the people who today are in control of the destiny of the French Republic."

Camillien Houde singled out the Canadians he held responsible for the order: left-wing bureaucrats in Ottawa. These bureaucrats, said the mayor, wanted to take advantage of the long Labour Day weekend in order to quietly get rid of Count de Bernonville. Houde added that Bernonville had been wounded 32 times and had received many war decorations and was a heroic figure. In addition, 20 other accused men living in Montreal risked the same tragic fate.

Meanwhile, the mayor of Montreal contacted William Leahy in Washington, President Truman's chief of staff at the White House. Leahy knew the Vichy régime well, since he had served there as American ambassador during the war. Houde urged him to come to the rescue of Bernonville. "My reason for contacting you," said the mayor, "can be explained by the fact that I belong to a French-speaking ethnic group, the only one on the continent, and we need the protection of powerful people in order to obtain justice." [1]

His message to the former ambassador was picked up by the press, but was not referred to again. On September 8, four days after sending his telegramme to Washington, Houde received an answer. Leahy curtly informed him that he had no intention of doing anything for Bernonville, had never met him, was not aware of the nature of the charges he was facing and in any case did not have the necessary authority toapply pressure on Canadian authorities. [2] Houde got a similar reply from Pierre Dupuy, a Canadian diplomat who had undertaken several missions in Vichy on behalf of the Allies.

The federal government seemed ill-prepared for the wind that was blowing in Quebec. Even in Montreal, immigration officials were generally cast in the Anglo-Saxon mould and therefore out of touch with reality in Quebec. Commissioner Smith of the Immigration department was questioned on the first day of the affair. He did not see why a man associated with Vichy and sentenced to death by French courts for collaboration should stay for long in Canada. The bureaucrat confirmed to the press that the federal government intended to deport Bernonville before Monday, that is in two days. Why make a change in customary procedure?

Things didn't turn out as Smith expected, however. As soon as the Bernonville family was arrested, lawyers set to work. Bernard Bourdon and Noël and Frédéric Dorion immediately explored the possibility of legal recourse. They succeeded in having the deportation order submitted to the Superior Court so that its validity could be judged. There was thus a chance of a reprieve for Bernonville and his family, who were still detained on rue St. Antoine.

The federal government was afraid of the political and highly explosive potential of the affair, and quickly began back-pedaling on the reasons motivating the deportation order. Two days after the mayor's declaration, Keenleyside, the deputy minister in charge of immigration in Ottawa, jumped into the ring and justified the decision of his bureaucrats with a less trenchant argument. Bernonville, he said, had probably assassinated several Canadian pilots during the German Occupation of France. Besides, his file revealed the murder of Canada's allies — members of the French Resistance. Finally, the deputy minister underlined the fact that France, the mother country of French Canadians, sought the return of Bernonville. Once he got back to France, he would receive a new trial.

The reply from Houde was swift as lightning:

"(...) your information must comes from the so-called 'purge trials' of the Fourth French Republic, in which very few French citizens still have any confidence, and to which the entire world, with the possible exception of Russia and her satellites, attaches no importance whatever." [3]

René Chaloult, a deputy in the provincial legislature, not only cast doubt on Keenleyside's information. Chaloult also discredited Keenleyside himself as "a fanatical, francophobic, anti-Catholic Freemason." [4]

From France a completely different version of Bernonville's past began to stream in, in the form of press dispatches. Although there were some inaccuracies here and there, the articles gave a reasonably accurate picture of the collaborationist past of Jacques de Bernonville. The anglophone and francophone press reproduced this information. It was learned that Bernonville had been sentenced to death in absentia in October 1947 by a court of justice in Toulouse. His activities at the head of the Phalange Africaine were outlined, as was his role in the repression of the Resistance on the Glières and Vercors plateaus. In short, the image of Bernonville provided in these articles was that of a willing auxiliary of the Nazis — and a war criminal. [5]

Starting on September 8, when the veil was being torn away from his true past, Bernonville told Mayor Houde who he thought was responsible for this campaign "of perfidious insinuations." Clearly, he

59

said, it was due to "the anti-Christian machinations of Communists and ... Jews."[6]

The former officer, still in detention on rue St. Antoine, was asked to respond to the dispatches arriving from Paris. He haughtily replied that the law of silence should be observed and indicated that the information was a tissue of lies.

On September 20, Bernonville and his family were released thanks to their good friend Jean Bonnel, who provided bail of $5,000. As far as immigration authorities were concerned, the deportation order was still in effect. Its implementation was only being delayed until the trial which, they hoped, would confirm that they had taken the right decision.

"LONG LIVE PÉTAIN STOP LONG LIVE BERNONVILLE"

From the beginning, petitions, the creation of defence committees, and pleas to the federal and French governments gave to the affair a highly political character. Within a few days, a Montreal resident named Barrière got 6,000 people to sign a petition asking the federal government to reverse its decision. Volunteers, like a certain Madame Racine, crisscrossed the city's streets with the petition in hand, and played up all the humanitarian pathos of the imminent deportation of this father of a family. The petition was sent to Ottawa, to the minister of external affairs Louis St. Laurent, who was soon to replace William Lyon Mackenzie King as Prime Minister of Canada.

The wave of sympathy soon flooded the whole province. In Quebec City, Dr. Philippe Hamel took up Count de Bernonville's defence in the press. Hamel was an unusual figure — more of a politician than a dentist. In 1935, he was a deputy in the provincial legislature representing a self-styled reformist party, the Action Libérale Nationale. The next year he crossed over to the Union Nationale of Maurice Duplessis. This new political organization was the result of the merger of the Quebec Conservative Party and the Action Libérale Nationale.

Once Duplessis, the head of the new party, was ensconced in office, he saw little need for waging battle alongside Hamel, who was something of a hotheaded ideologue. Indeed, Hamel had built a reputation over the previous few years as the arch-enemy of the electricity trusts and the denouncer of the evils of capitalism.

Hamel was disappointed and withdrew for a time from active political life. But during the war he participated in the birth of the Bloc Populaire Canadien. This party was created in order to give voice to the resentment felt by French Canadians during the conscription crisis of 1942. Along with Paul Gouin and René Chaloult, Hamel planned to use this new platform in order to continue the struggle for the nationalization of electrical utilities. However, internal differences divided the newly-created party, which disintegrated a few years later, in 1948.

Hamel's nationalism was marked by the notion of the survival of the French-Canadian "race". Such a man could not remain indifferent to politics. In 1948, he was ready to take the leap once again. He worked in the campaign organization of his friend René Chaloult, and like Chaloult he got deeply involved in the Bernonville affair. On September 7, in a declaration to the press, he said he saw nothing criminal in the action of Count de Bernonville during the Occupation. All Bernonville had done was act under the orders of France's legitimate government.[7]

A few days later, in Montreal, a committee for the defence of Bernonville took over from the informal group which had launched the petition campaign. Called the "Committee for the Defence of French Political Refugees", the group was led by a former Bloc Populaire Canadien candidate, Paul Massé. The organizer of the petition, L.-A. Barrière, also joined the group. As soon as it was created, the organization resorted to the Rougier thesis developed three years beforehand, according to which Pétain was an astute strategist who mystified the German thugs in order to help the Allied cause. According to the committee, Bernonville had simply obeyed Vichy's orders and followed in the footsteps of the Marshal.

In its appeal to the French government, the committee associated Bernonville even more closely with the prisoner of Ile d'Yeu. In both cases, Bernonville and Pétain were victims of the excesses of the Fourth Republic. To Georges Bidault they wrote:

"Give back to us, give back to the entire world, the right to unreservedly admire your fatherland. Lower the gates, open wide the doors of your prisons. Liberate the Marshal, the oldest prisoner in the world, and the thousands of political prisoners who are still victims of persistent hatred."[8]

The committee recruited mainly among the members of the nationalist intelligentsia who had been involved in the Bloc Populaire

Canadien or who had felt some kinship with the Union Nationale. Almost all of them claimed to be autonomists. During the war, some had been well-known supporters of Pétain. The Bernonville affair gave them a chance to give vent once more to their feelings, especially since there was no longer any need to support Allied war aims.

The organization was directed in Quebec City by René Chaloult and Philippe Hamel, and in Montreal by Camillien Houde and Robert Rumilly. The columnist Richard Daigneault called them "The gang of four", since he felt they were a noisy little group of nationalists trying to pass themselves off as the voice of Quebec itself.

Indeed, a Quebec city notary, Gustave Jobidon, claimed to speak for all French Canadians when he addressed a very explicit telegram to Robert Schuman and the French government:

"French Canadians outraged by deportation Count de Bernonville. French Republic dishonored by ingratitude toward authentic hero. Anti-French campaign here if deportation and assassination take place stop humiliation for us. Long live Pétain stop long live Bernonville." [9]

The committee could not count however on the open support of Quebec Premier Maurice Duplessis, even though he was an ardent defender of Quebec autonomy. Duplessis acted like a sly fox throughout the affair, letting some of his deputies get involved, but keeping in a state of alert himself, as if he wanted to carefully assess the electoral potential of the affair. After all, provincial elections had just taken place.

Despite the wait-and-see attitude of the head of the Quebec government, the movement well knew that Duplessis was sympathetic. In addition, by way of support, some ministers in the Quebec provincial cabinet promised to send the committee a check for several thousand dollars.

One of the jobs of the newly-constituted committee was to create a common front among French-Canadian associations. Pressures were exerted on the federal government in the form of letters sent to Louis St. Laurent. The Maisonneuve council of the Knights of Columbus urged the federal government not to hand over "His Excellency the Count, a great Catholic patriot, to the French Communists." [10] The Jeunesse organization of Rosemont used the same theme when it urged the Canadian government to be clement, and prevent this "anti-Communist from being delivered to the French Communists." [11]

Philippe Hamel personally wrote to Louis St. Laurent on September 21, asking for clemency in Bernonville's case. In a confidential letter addressed to the minister, he even opened a whole debate on the issue of immigration. Hamel had been a devoted Pétainist during the war, and now showed the full strength of his Pétainist convictions:

"We could recruit first-class immigrants in the prisons of France just now. That is where most of the élite which has not already fled to Canada, the United States or South America can be found. I am sorry if I shock you by expressing such an idea."[12]

And Hamel went on to say that

"(...) in spite of his mistakes, the greatest citizen of France during World War Two was Marshal Pétain. He was sentenced to death by a parody of justice, with the complicity of the French and the English, just as Saint Joan of Arc was burnt at the stake by an iniquitous court, to the great satisfaction of the English and the French."

ON THE RADIO AND IN THE NEWSPAPERS

The Bernonville affair received substantial coverage on the radio and in newspapers in Quebec during Fall 1948. Editorial-writers quickly divided into two distinct groups, which just about perfectly reflected the wartime cleavage between Vichy supporters and Gaullists. Defending Count de Bernonville were Catholic and national French-language newspapers, such as *Montréal-Matin*, *La Patrie*, *L'action catholique* and *Le Devoir*.

In its portrayal of Jacques de Bernonville, the Montreal newspaper *La Patrie* did mention the fact that he had been responsible for the maintenance of order in Lyon during the Occupation. The article then took a completely different tack, saying that Count de Bernonville had been duly appointed by Marshal Pétain and "executed French laws against Communist terrorists and had several of them shot to death."[13]

For his part, Roger Duhamel launched a broadside at the French Resistance. The publisher of *Montréal-Matin*, a faithful reflection of the thinking of the Union Nationale, wrote: "(...) French Communists carefully took control of all hotbeds of the Resistance to the enemy. They elevated terrorism into a system."[14] For Duhamel, the work of the French purge trials had been used as a vast operation to eliminate political adversaries. For this reason, he concluded, Bernonville could deservedly be considered "a political refugee" and therefore deserved the sympathy of Canadian authorities.

In the September 10 issue of the Quebec City newspaper *L'action catholique*, Louis-Philippe Roy cast doubt on the very French legal system that had to judge the responsibility of the count during the war: "Is the French justice system in a position to fairly judge this political prisoner? By every account, the climate does not seem to be favourable." Apart from a few traitors, wrote Alonzo Cinq-Mars in *La Patrie*, most people currently jailed or shot for Collaboration with the Nazis were only obeying the Vichy government, which was legitimate and legally constituted. Bernonville fell into this last group.

In the September 7 issue of *Le Devoir*, under the heading "Bloc-Notes," a piece bearing the initials P.S. (Paul Sauriol) also cast doubt on the value of a new trial:

"People talk of a new trial for Mr. Bernonville; if that trial is anything like those of Marshal Pétain and Pierre Laval, then it isn't worth the trouble. The Canadian government should not look into the merit of the question, but into the circumstances. Mr. de Bernonville ought to be granted asylum, the way Canada has recently granted asylum to other refugees."

In an editorial signed by André Laurendeau, *Le Devoir* came back to the affair on September 11. Laurendeau, a former MP of the Bloc Populaire, said that Bernonville should be seen as "a political refugee". He said there was no justification for the reaction of French authorities, even if Bernonville had illegally entered the country with forged papers. "To flatly invoke the letter of immigration regulations is to hypocritically refuse the 'right to asylum' which is so often accorded to refugees." *Le Devoir* then drew from the right-wing French newspaper *Paroles françaises*, to aim its first arrows at Bernonville's adversaries, who were also presented as adversaries of Pétain. On September 25, in a "Bloc-Notes" written once again by Paul Sauriol, readers learned that "(...) the former adversaries of Vichy who see Fascists everywhere want us to believe that French public opinion is unanimous in condemning the Marshal and all those who followed him."

This point of view was shared by *Montréal-Matin*. In fact, a few days beforehand, on September 8, Roger Duhamel had written: "We should have expected as much; those who, throughout the war, told the

Few public photos remain of Jacques Dugé de Bernonville. Here, in February 1949, at the Kerhulu restaurant in Quebec City, he prepares his defense before the a deportation hearing at the Department of Immigration.

Accompanied by his friend Jean Bonnel, Jacques Dugé de Bernonville leaves the Montreal Immigration building on St. Antoine street, after having been ordered deported to France. The Montreal Herald headlined the story, ON WAY TO FIRING SQUAD? as he had been sentenced to death in absentia for treason. He appealed the deportation order.

1951. Bernonville, looking sardonically glum, rallies his friends around his cause.

January 1955. Bernonville leaves Montreal, one step ahead of deportation. Rather than face a firing squad in France, he chose exile in Brazil, where he was assassinated in 1972 after announcing his decision to write his memoirs.

tall stories of the Left and rejoiced in countless acts of infamy performed under the cover of 'resistentialism' have now resolutely taken position against Count de Bernonville."

Duhamel continued in the same vein, saying that the affair "was dripping with persistent hatred for the Vichy government, France's legal régime and one with which the United States and Canada maintained constant diplomatic relations."

On one point, the publisher of *Montréal-Matin* was, ironically, in agreement with the detractors of Count de Bernonville. That point was that the wartime cleavage in Canada between Vichy supporters and Gaullists was being reproduced in the Bernonville affair.

Le Canada, a federalist Montreal-based newspaper controlled by the Liberal Party of Canada, wrote on September 9:

"Just as was to be expected, everything that Quebec has in the way of fascist sympathizers, pro-Krauts and would-be collaborators during the war are now in the front ranks of the Bernonville affair. They are the very ones who did their best, during the war, to sabotage our war effort (...).

"It should moreover be noted that those who today are against Count de Bernonville's being handed over to the French justice system are the same ones who throughout the war applauded the Vichy régime (of which Bernonville was a part), when it delivered up to Franco those Spanish Republicans who had sought refuge in France and even had fought for France before Pétain signed the armistice. Their concept of 'the sacred right of asylum' certainly does vary, according to the circumstances and the people involved!"

This black-and-white vision of the affair needs some explanation. Those French Canadians who were opposed to de Gaulle in 1940, who "tolerated" him and who supported Vichy did not throw themselves in Hitler's arms. On the contrary, they accepted Canada's war aims when it came to Germany and sometimes paid lip service to those aims) although, when it came to the means to be used, some of them fiercely fought Conscription.

In French Canada during the war, there was no movement to support Hitler or the Nazi cause. With the May 1940 arrests of the Fascist Adrien Arcand and the main pro-Nazi leaders (all of them members of a national Canadian party), whatever sympathy for Hitler, no matter how feeble, was cut short.

Reality is far more complex. However, once the sort of exaggerations in *Le Canada* started coming out, the positions of both sides hardened into traditional antagonistic positions on Vichy.

In short, few editorial-writers in the French-Canadian press were willing to rise in support of the federal deportation order. Those who did, above all in *Le Canada*, followed the line established by the party in power in Ottawa. Moreover, the previous positions of these editorial-writers on clericalism and nationalism kept them at a critical distance from the Bernonville affair. Since the Bernonville cause was defended by their adversaries, that cause was therefore suspect.

According to *Le Canada*, the defenders of Count de Bernonville were more Pétainist that anyone who could be found in France and were among those seeking to weaken Canadian Confederation and the Liberal Party of Canada. Pétainism was dead in France, Eugène l'Heureux wrote, so it should be dead here as well.[15]

The newspaper opened its pages wide to those who wished to see Bernonville sent back to France to be judged. Canadian and French veterans expressed their dismay. The president of the Canadian Legion of the province of Quebec spoke on behalf of his members on September 11, and asked that the affair not be turned into a political battle. He urged that the question whether Bernonville had the right to stay in Canada should be left in the hands of the Canadian justice system.

A group of French veterans was much more outspoken and offered an absurd view of the consequences of supporting a Nazi collaborator like Bernonville.

"Finally, we demand the return of the concentration camps, the torture, the Gestapo and the gas chambers for which Bernonville and his heroes valiantly fought.

"Long live Pétain, long live Laval, long live Hitler, long live the Third Reich, down with the United Nations."[16]

On the whole, the veterans strengthened the ranks of the adversaries of Count de Bernonville, in what seemed fated to be an unequal struggle. Unlike the general public, these veterans had a good knowledge of the war. There was one exception, however, that confused the issue and bolstered those who believed they were sincerely supporting a father and a family in distress.

Captain Antoine Masson, a Canadian taken prisoner at the abortive Dieppe raid in August 1942, said he owed his escape from the clutches of the Germans to Bernonville. He said the organizers of his escape claimed to be acting on orders from the count. This account was quickly discounted, when it was suggested that the name of Bernonville might have been used by the Resistance for its own purposes. His name might have been used as a clever security precaution, in order to cover up the tracks if ever Masson was recaptured by the Germans.

The Masson story did not change the course of the affair, any more than the denunciation of Bernonville with regard to the murder in France of a Canadian pilot named Benoit. According to this account, the chief milicien supposedly used the dead pilot's identity papers in order to get into Canada. The most plausible hypothesis remains the explication given by Bernonville, when he swore he used the name Benoit out of devotion to his patron saint Benoit.

The English-language press rose in unison against Bernonville. English-language newspapers had been Gaullist during the war and were now against Bernonville after the war. All the editorials written at the beginning of September in Montreal's anglophone newspapers were in the same vein. All unanimously demanded that political pressures to keep Bernonville in Canada cease and desist. All said that it was important to trust the justice system to deal with the matter. In any case, a trial would soon determine whether or not Bernonville had the right to remain in the country.

The Montreal Herald accepted Paris's version of the facts surrounding the French fugitive, and in its September 8, 1948 issue categorized Bernonville's supporters as ranging from Fascists to nationalists.

For its part, *The Standard* published on September 11 a photocopy of French police files on Bernonville. Dated January 1945, the search warrant listed crimes committed by Bernonville, namely: arbitrary arrest, breach of state security, theft, violence, etc. The newspapers got their information from Jokelson, who had been the first to recognize Bernonville, in Granby. In the French-language press, this information was also reproduced by *Le Petit Journal*. However, this type of document was generally considered in French Canada to be propaganda developed by the French purge trials.

In Quebec City, the *Quebec Chronicle-Telegraph* launched into Camillien Houde and Philippe Hamel, whom it accused of misleading the public. The newspaper said that a collaborationist should not be mistaken for a political prisoner. If Bernonville had indeed illegally entered the country, then he should be deported back to the country from whence he came.

In the federal capital, meanwhile, *The Ottawa Citizen* maintained that the court ruling on Bernonville, made in October 1947 in Toulouse, came long after the settling of accounts that immediately followed the war. No matter what Bernonville's defenders might say, France's justice system was in good shape. The editorial-writer noted that if the information transmitted by Paris was accurate, Bernonville was not some sort of political refugee, but a war criminal instead.

Radio stations also got involved in the media campaign surrounding the Bernonville affair. On September 12, Robert Rumilly sat in front of the microphone to deliver the first in a series of talks broadcast throughout the affair. Speaking in his quickfire way, the pamphleteer and historian tried to convince his listeners that the treatment of this Christian and Frenchman was disgraceful.

He attacked from every direction and managed to hit home. Rumilly singled out the language of work used by Immigration officials, who were the cause of Bernonville's problems, citing one example in particular:

"I had the curiosity to walk through the immense building that houses the Immigration services in Ottawa. (...)There you will see hundreds of bureaucrats. Look for any French Canadians, look hard and count them. In fact, in all the offices of the federal administration, the French language can only be heard during one hour in each day: that hour is seven in the morning, the hour of the cleaning-ladies." [17]

For Rumilly, there was someone above the bureaucrats. The person ultimately responsible was Louis St. Laurent, head of the Liberal Party of Canada and slated to become the next Prime Minister. Rumilly did the rounds of Quebec and noted that the members of the Liberal Party were the only French Canadians not to support Bernonville. Would St. Laurent be more forgiving if a person of Jewish origin were involved? During the war, Rumilly insinuated, the minister had taken no time in releasing a certain Fred Rose, alias Fred Rosenberg, who had been arrested by the police for espionage. "Mr. St. Laurent," said Rumilly, "do not deport this other man whom your police have arrested and whose name is not Sam Cohen or Fred Rosenberg but Jacques de Bernonville."[18]

CAMILLIEN, NOUS VOILÀ!

By the end of September 1948, the Bernonville affair really got moving, thanks above all to the efforts of the mayor of Montreal, Camillien Houde, who had literally created the affair. From the very beginning, he indicated to his fellow citizens what they ought to think about the affair. The public was well-disposed to him and his words crossed the Atlantic.

From this moment onward, Houde received a large amount of letters. On the whole, his voters and other people living outside of the city encouraged him to continue. According to the notary Lachapelle of St. François du Lac, in Yamaska county, "half of the French population was Communist and ought to be killed — well before Jacques."[19]

Dr. Michaud, a physician, greatly appreciated the courage of the mayor and noted that in this affair "the actions of Canadian ministers were dictated by England."[20] Conrad Bérubé of Montreal brought up the same theme: the people who had interned Houde during the war, that is the little gang from Ottawa, were the same actors in the Bernonville drama.[21]

Joseph Valois, a Houde supporter, thanked him warmly for what he had accomplished. "Count de Bernonville, as you know, is one of the right-hand men of the great Pétain, and his ungrateful country has exiled him in this great ideological struggle."[22] Valois concluded his letter by repeating that he admired Houde for having spared no effort in the election campaign to fight Communism.

An anglophone resident of St. Laurent, in the Montreal suburbs, also supported the mayor. If English blood had flowed in the Count's veins, wrote Leo Meehan, then he would never have had any problems with federal authorities. It just happens that Bernonville was French.[23]

The mayor of Montreal got a big boost when he received a newspaper cutting praising Count de Bernonville's military record in World War One. This precious document was sent by none other than abbé Félix-Antoine Savard, the author of *Menaud, maître-draveur*, a classic of French-Canadian literature. Houde thanked him warmly and quickly informed Rumilly about this fortunate surprise.

Among the letters received, some were written by members of the French colony in Montreal, and expressed their support in vehement terms. They were generally anonymous and were from devoted supporters of the Marshal, some of whom had likely compromised themselves by collaborating in France during the Occupation. Here is a passage from one of the letters, in which a group of the Marshal's partisans, installed in Montreal, explain their struggle:

"FOR FRANCE, FOR CATHOLICISM, AGAINST COMMUNISM.

"This is the traditional struggle of the province of Quebec. These people could well have left for Argentina, Brazil, Venezuela or elsewhere. They came to Quebec because they want to remain French and they want their children and their grandchildren to remain French.

"Because these people who exposed themselves, fought for the ideal of the regeneration of France and the world, and wanted to settle in the one country in the world with the healthiest and purest values." [24]

Another group, or perhaps the same one but using a different name, congratulated Jean Bonnel and Camillien Houde for publicizing the scandal. That was an extraordinarily intelligent thing to do. "Riffraff are always afraid of public opinion when their own crimes are uncovered." [25] Houde and Bonnel could count on these supporters. "You have the support of all pure Frenchmen and they are legion," declared the authors, who called themselves the Vigilance group. They mentioned however that they were afraid some of their careless compatriots might be uncovered by French consular services in Montreal. During the last year, the authors of the letter stated, the security measures observed up till then by some members of the French colony in Montreal had been loosened. Such fools ran the risk of being detected, particularly at monthly meetings of the French colony.

One Frenchman, Jean Dufour, had arrived in Canada in March 1948 with his six children, and castigated his country "where you are called 'filthy viper' if you are anti-Communist and 'collaborator' if you don't like the English..." [26] Dufour then went on to call Bernonville's opponents, a "collection of rogues and Apaches plotting our downfall."

Those Frenchmen writing to Houde were not an accurate reflection of their entire community, however. At the beginning of the affair, for example, one of the French supporters of the count tried to have members of the Union Nationale Française of Montreal sign his petition. That didn't work, since the members of the association refused to sign.

In short, support for the mayor flooded in from all over and rare were the letters opposing his actions. Élisabeth de Courval wrote from New York where she was then located, that she regretted Houde's intervention without approving Pétain's imprisonment. "(...) that is no reason," she wrote, "to launch a campaign of hatred against our mother country."[27]

A certain Madame Arthur Salvas, of Lachine, also expressed her dissatisfaction to the mayor:

> "It seems to me that you ought to have enough to do managing the city's affairs, without intervening in decisions of the French government. Particularly since, on this side of the Atlantic, we are poorly informed and not very knowledgeable about certain French people."[28]

An anglophone lady did not mince words in condemning the attitude of the mayor. She lumped Fascists and nationalists together, and wrongly considered Adrien Arcand to be the master manipulator of the affair. In a sarcastic tone, Mrs. Silverstone asked that Houde's friends check the legality of every Jewish family's entry into Canada.[29]

Camillien Houde's declarations in favor of Jacques de Bernonville traveled quickly. A few days later, they reached France via the right-wing press of that country. Many readers found the news from Quebec very pleasing, and let the mayor know.

Among them was a Frenchman in hiding who admitted he could not identify himself. With something like 20 other individuals, he was on the list of people like Bernonville being pursued.

He gave his message a strangely Gaullist title: "A Frenchman speaks to the courageous French Canadians."[30] His appeal to French Canadians aimed to thank them for helping the Frenchmen being tracked down in Canada and to incite them to continue their campaign, using "all legal and even extra-legal methods."

Another writer spoke of the "absolutely correct" attitude of German authorities in Paris during the war, and sighed that "the only consolation at the present time is to see French-speaking countries like yours raise voices which cannot be raised here." [31]

The Thermidor group wrote to the mayor of Montreal that it was waiting for H Hour of the counter-revolution, which would come at the appropriate moment and rid France of the Soviets and their proxies. These authors described themselves as the pure ones, and called on the mayor to do everything in his power to prevent Bernonville's return to France, since he faced immediate and certain death. It was better to wait for this hour "of liberty and justice to ring the death-knell of the so-called Resistance and of these so-called heroes and liberators." [32]

Houde replied to all of these people (at least when he had their address). To the French, he explained the fact that French Canadians were anxiously waiting the outcome of the situation on the other side of the Atlantic. His people, surrounded by 160 million anglophones, hoped they could count on the support of France in resisting this environment. The mayor of Montreal shared their desire to see France rise once again. [33]

FOOTNOTES

1. Text of the telegramme sent by Camillien Houde to Admiral William Leahy (Washington), early September 1948 (RR; ANQ; 14).

2. Telegramme from William Leahy to Camillien Houde, September 8, 1948 (RR; ANQ; 14).

3. *Montréal-Matin*, September 7, 1948.

4. *La Presse*, September 13, 1948.

6. Letter from Jacques de Bernonville to Camillien Houde, September 8, 1948 (RR; ANQ; 14).

7. *Montréal-Matin*, September 7, 1948.

8. Statement sent by the Committee for the Defence of French Political Refugees to Georges Bidault, France, Fall 1948 (RR; ANQ; 12).

9. *Le Canada*, September 15, 1948.

10. Letter from the Maisonneuve chapter of the Knights of Columbus to the Justice Department, Ottawa, September 9, 1948 (DB; ANC).

11. Letter from Gérard Deguire on behalf of the Jeunesse group of Rosemont, to the Justice Department, Ottawa, September 7, 1948 (DB; ANC).

12. Letter from Philippe Hamel to Louis St. Laurent, September 21, 1948 (RR; ANQ; 14).

13. *La Patrie*, September 5, 1948.

14. *Montréal-Matin*, September 7, 1948.

15. *Le Canada*, September 20, 1948.

16. Ibid., September 13, 1948.

17. Notes for a radio talk given by Robert Rumilly entitled "A principle is at stake in the Bernonville affair", Fall 1948 (RR; ANQ; 12).

18. Ibid.

19. Letter from J.-Er. Lachapelle to Camillien Houde, Fall 1948 (RR; ANQ; 14).

20. Letter from J. B. Michaud to Camillien Houde, September 14, 1948 (RR; ANQ; 14).

21. Letter from Conrad Bérubé to Camillien Houde, September 14, 1948 (RR; ANQ; 14).

22. Letter from Joseph de Valois to Camillien Houde, September 6, 1948 (RR; ANQ; 14).

23. Letter from Leo Meehan to Camillien Houde, September 12, 1948 (RR; ANQ; 14).

24. Letter from an anonymous Montreal-based group of the Marshal's supporters to Camillien Houde, September 1948 (RR; ANQ; 14).

25. Letter from the anonymous so-called "Vigilance" group to Jean Bonnel, September 6, 1948 (RR; ANQ; 14).

26. Letter from Jean Dufour to Camillien Houde, September 9, 1948 (RR; ANQ; 14).

27. Letter from Élisabeth de Courval, New York, to Camillien Houde, September 19, 1948 (RR; ANQ; 14).

28. Letter from Mrs. Arthur Salvas to Camillien Houde, September 7, 1948 (RR; ANQ; 14).

29. Letter from Mrs. Silverstone to Camillien Houde, early September 1948 (RR; ANQ; 14).

30. Anonymous letter sent to Camillien Houde by a Frenchman being tracked down, early September 1948 (RR; ANQ; 14).

31. Anonymous letter from a Parisian to Camillien Houde, September 8, 1948.

32. Letter from the so-called "Thermidor" group to Camillien Houde, September 22, 1948 (RR; ANQ; 14).

33. Letter from abbé P. Régis (Montpellier) to Camillien Houde, November 10, 1948 (RR; ANQ; 14).

CHAPTER V

A national affair

On October 15, 1948, the Bernonville took on national dimensions. It was revealed that federal cabinet orders-in-council existed, for the purpose of allowing four French fugitives to remain in the country. Bernonville's trial was taking place that fall. The story of the four fugitives resembled that of Bernonville and gave the protagonists the chance to continue talking about the Bernonville affair without really going into the details.

On that day, the Toronto daily newspaper *The Globe & Mail* divulged the presence in Canada of four more French collaborators. They were: Georges Montel, 49 years of age, Julien Labedan, 39, André Boussat and Jean Louis Huc, both 45. The four had come into the country with forged passports.

It was learned that a Liberal senator had been manoeuvring for the last year and a half in the hopes of obtaining a permanent residency visa. The senator in question, Jean-Marie Dessureault, openly admitted in the article that he had received support from the clergy for this purpose. Eminent members of the Catholic hierarchy had recommended and strongly supported the four requests for visas.

In addition, he said, to make his actions seem more credible, the future Prime Minister, Louis St. Laurent, was personally aware of the special authorization these individuals had received. Indeed, the prime minister had attended a cabinet meeting in September, when the orders-in-council were issued.

These decisions had been made quietly. Labedan had fully informed Rumilly two weeks after the beginning of the Bernonville affair. Labedan had seen in the government move the crowning glory of "the struggle we waged for the revered leader who would have restored the full grandeur of France."[1] Actually, what really happened was that the federal government feared it would have five "Bernonville affairs" to deal with at the same time. Besides, it should be noted that the bishops of Quebec were the key players; they had been clearly told that they could find a way out for the increasing numbers of French fugitives in hiding. The fugitives' defenders were under the strictest orders not to make waves.

Everywhere in the country, the English-language press was in an uproar over the way the federal government had acted. With *The Globe & Mail* in the lead, English-language newspapers denounced the secret orders. *The Globe* blankly referred to the four Frenchmen as "collaborators". Three days after the orders were uncovered, the newspaper demanded in an editorial that the Canadian government offer a full explanation.

On October 19, the newspaper mentioned that Alistair Stewart, an MP with the Co-operative Commonwealth Federation (CCF), planned to fight a battle in the next session of the federal Parliament if the government did not come clean by then. He said that the orders-in-council seemed all the less justified, since seven people of Jewish origin had just been deported to Germany because their passports were not in order.

In Montreal, English-language newspapers followed the lead of *The Globe & Mail. The Standard* said nothing indicated that the records of these men were clean. Moreover, the federal cabinet had to clarify its position on the safe-conducts issued. The *Star* said much the same, and demanded that the government provide full information about the affair. *The Gazette* detected a lack of openness in the democratic process and an act of manipulation. Finally, *The Herald* wondered about the mysterious aspects of the affair and the secrecy surrounding the government's handling of the affair.[2]

At the same time, *The Herald* began publishing a series of three articles on the Milice in France, in order to make clear the difference between the French Milice and the Canadian reserve that bore the same name ("Militia"). The newspaper invited a decorated veteran of the French Resistance living in Montreal to share his experiences. The latter (it was possibly Jokelson or Michel Pichard) described the struggle of the Resistance against the Milice, as well as the tortures inflicted by the Milice during the Occupation. Finally, this Resistance veteran mentioned Vichy's violent treatment of Jews.

In general, the news that orders-in-council had been issued led to a completely different reaction in the French-Canadian press. From this moment onward, the debate suddenly changed course. The turmoil in the media took on two new dimensions. On the one hand, the affair moved closer to Ottawa and caught the attention of newspapers across the country. On the other hand, starting on October 15, the controversy came to be interpreted as part of the well-known antagonism between Canada's two main linguistic groups. French-Canadian editorial-writers made this shift in their interpretation.

On October 19, a few days after the existence of the cabinet orders-in-council was revealed, Alonzo Cinq-Mars wrote in *La Patrie*:

"All the noise being made about French refugees who have arrived on our shores is also likely to harm other French citizens, former partisans of the Vichy government, who might wish to settle in our country. And there remain many of them."

The same day, the publisher of *Montréal-Matin*, Roger Duhamel, came to the rescue this time of the federal government and praised the measures taken in the case of the four Frenchmen. He said that the commotion over the cabinet orders showed that "the enemies of Marshal Pétain and of the Vichy régime were having a new fit of hysterics." In fact, the war undertaken by English-language newspapers and particularly *The Globe & Mail* was "a new sign of anti-French fanaticism." The accusation had been made and *Le Devoir* took it up and developed it further.

As for André Laurendeau, editorial-writer at *Le Devoir*, he quite rightfully saw that the uproar over the four refugees was an indirect but flagrant response to the campaign launched the previous month on behalf of Count de Bernonville. However, he dodged the main point by suggesting that the uproar could by a "reply to the new attitude of the government when it comes to French immigrants."[3]

French citizens had only begun to be admitted to Canada following the same administrative procedures as were applied to citizens of the British Commonwealth. That is what Laurendeau was referring to. According to him, francophobic bureaucrats, working hand in hand with like-minded English-language newspapers, divulged information about the cabinet orders out of frustration over the adoption of new immigration policies. Laurendeau said, however, that the four individuals were not collaborators but bureaucrats of the Pétain régime, a perfectly legitimate régime.

This diversion of the affair for nationalist ends went further. A link had been established between the affair of the collaborators, on the one hand, and the attitude of a very "British" administration with its Anglo-Saxon ideals and lack of sensitivity toward francophones, on the other hand; this link would be long-lasting. The new approach helped Rumilly develop more sophisticated arguments and more powerful rhetoric.

Two days later, on October 20, Gérard Filion wrote a long editorial in the same vein. The publisher of *Le Devoir* predicted that in the future all French citizens arriving in Canada would be suspected of Nazism or Communism in the eye of the anglophones in the Immigration department and the press. Filion charged that it was a new strategy to block the arrival of French immigrants in Canada. He then issued this warning:

"If Canada refuses the right of asylum to these people persecuted for their political opinions, it will be eloquent proof that civilization and Christian charity have made no progress since the last war...."

Le Devoir waited a few days and then returned to the affair on October 22, under the signature this time of Paul Sauriol. He concluded that the campaign led by the English-language press was "inspired by more and more overt racism." The newspaper blasted the English press and bureaucracy, the Canadian Legion, the CCF and the Quebec section of the Communist Party, all of which had taken position against Bernonville.

The conflict between Quebec supporters and adversaries of the collaborators caused some institutions to keep their distance from all the fuss. Catherine de Bernonville was temporarily suspended from the Collège Marie-de-France. The school's board of directors not very convincingly explained it had decided to suspended the student because of the risk of tuberculosis in the Bernonville family. On October 21, an anonymous writer in *Le Devoir*, under the pseudonym Hippocrates ridiculed the school's position.

The liberal French-language press stood alone in its combat against the presumed collaborators. For example, *Le Canada* was the first newspaper along with *The Globe & Mail* to have revealed on October 15 the existence of secret orders-in-council.

Le Canada, the official organ of the Liberal Party, was upset that the four Frenchmen were being allowed to stay, and temporarily took its distance from the government in Ottawa. After all, the Liberals were the ones to have signed the secret orders.

On October 21, the newspaper warned its compatriots of the risk of damaging French Canada's reputation if attempts continued to offer asylum to the fugitives. "Three and a half million French Canadians would have to put up with the North American accusation of being 'fascist' for having sought to keep a half dozen suspects in Quebec." Even so, the suspects would manage to stay in the country. During the darkest moments of the controversy, the federal government would refer back to the September 1948 orders-in-council. But then, the four other fugitives did not have quite as spectacular a collaborationist past as Jacques be Bernonville.

JOKELSON TRACKED DOWN

Suspicions over the identity of the person responsible for the leaked information quickly led to Jokelson. A month beforehand, *Le Petit Journal* had published photocopies of Bernonville's arrest warrant, along with *The Standard*. Then, on October 17, *Le Petit Journal* revealed its source. "There is every reason to believe that the person who denounced Count de Bernonville is a Jew by the name of J., who has lived in Montreal for some time, where he heads an export company." [4]

Around the same time, a confidential memo reached one of the highest public-security officials in Quebec. The message bore neither address nor signature, but was probably intended for Hilaire Beauregard, the big boss of the provincial police. There was no doubt who had written the memo: it was none other than the mayor of Montreal, Camillien Houde.

Houde informed the director of the police that Bernonville had received a little coffin, accompanied by a death threat. According to the count, the package had surely come from Jokelson, a representative of the Dreyfus firm. The mayor added that Jokelson was likely the person who had provided the Canadian government and even the French embassy in Ottawa with all the information published in the newspapers about Jacques de Bernonville.

The mayor said that some way should be found to incriminate this individual. After all, he insinuated, the fact Jokelson worked for a company with offices in all major cities around the world could provide an excellent cover for French police informers.

> "As I asked you above, would you submit this case to the appropriate person, and if you received a directive allowing you to open an investigation of the activities of this sinister individual, you might be able to establish that he sent a death threat, a concealed one possibly, but a death threat nonetheless..." [5]

Camillien Houde shrewdly explained the reason for sending his memo to the official: it would be hard for him to directly use his own police services. He deplored the fact that the powers he currently had did not allow him to order his chief of police to open an investigation for the moment. In conclusion, Houde wrote:

> "As a result, I am contacting you as my last chance to protect poor de Bernonville at least during his trial and until a judgment is rendered. Personally, if someone sends me a coffin, don't trouble yourself, I think I will be able to track it down on my own."

It is hard to find out what happened after that. There is however a very revealing unsigned note among the Robert Rumilly papers in Montreal.[6] Hilaire Beauregard, says the memo, apparently put a detective in charge of the anti-Communist squad on Jokelson's tail. Once the results of the investigation were known, the head of the provincial police had to inform the people interested in the affair.

NO EXTRADITION REQUESTED

The French diplomatic corps was informed by Jokelson and others of the presence of Jacques de Bernonville in Canada, but reacted with ambivalence.

Within the consulate in Montreal, there seems to have been a difference of opinion between the consul, Ernest Triat, who never failed to invite Count de Bernonville to social receptions, and the vice-consul, Pierre Gabard. Rumilly was informed of Gabard's position by a young student, Jean-Marc Léger, who knew Chantal, one of Jacques de Bernonville's daughters, well. Léger sympathized with the cause of the Bernonvilles and wanted to help the family. On October 5, Léger repeated to Rumilly what Gabard had said to one of his colleagues.

During a meeting, the vice-consul of France in Montreal was said to have portrayed Bernonville in a terrible light, "accusing him of the most atrocious crimes and executions."[7] The students presented these facts to Rumilly and suggested that the historian might ask the vice-consul "to back up accusations that were gratuitous to say the least."

In Ottawa, the French embassy kept silent about the affair for six weeks. Francisque Gay, the ambassador, had been appointed less than a year beforehand by President Vincent Auriol. Francisque Gay was a veteran of the Resistance and more of a journalist at heart than a diplomat, although, because of his first name (which was also the name of Vichy's highest decoration) he was subjected to all sorts of puns.

On October 20, the ambassador broke his silence and declared to everyone's astonishment that France had never asked Canada to extradite anyone. Even more surprising was his appeal to the fugitives to return to France where they would be assured of new trials.

The next day, the ambassador left Ottawa for Montreal, where he gave a highly unusual press conference before 50 journalists gathered at the Windsor Hotel. There he again stated the position of the French government, which had never requested extradition. Above all, Gay defended the legal system of his country which had been attacked so often by French-Canadian newspapers. He made a stirring demonstration of the worth of France's justice system.

Francisque Gay was asked what could explain the fact that the French government had made no formal request. He indicated that Montreal newspapers were the explanation. At the same time, the ambassador may have provided a key to understanding the French government's silence:

> "I will tell you a secret. Not even a memo has been exchanged on the subject between my government and the embassy. This is hardly the time to request an extradition, particularly in view of the campaign undertaken by Montreal newspapers..."[8]

Ambassador Gay's public statement heated up the atmosphere once again. The same day that the ambassador spoke out, a Montreal resident, Alvarez Tousignant, wrote him an intimidating personal letter. Tousignant accused the diplomat of forgetting Christian charity and of secretly plotting with sinister individuals in order to hurt Count de Bernonville. He finished his furious letter with a vehement attack on the ambassador for using the term 'collaborator' to refer to the Frenchmen in question. "It is absolutely odious to speak of collaborators, in Canada, when these men courageously served their legal government, a government moreover that was recognized by our country."[9]

In *Montréal-Matin*, Roger Duhamel cast doubt on the strength of Gay's convictions during the time he had served in the Resistance. Duhamel suggested that the ambassador might have played both sides during the Occupation, but sarcastically did not blame him for that. The newspaper publisher wrote, clearly in bad faith, that Gay's ambiguity was much like that of a great patriot who had acted in the same way, namely Philippe Pétain.

In Mégantic, far from Montreal, Jean Tavernier did not believe the "honey-sweet" claims of the ambassador. According to the editorial-writer of the *Mégantic*, "the purge trials have killed too many real Frenchmen, whose only fault was and remains their well-known anti-Communism."[10]

In France, the weekly *Samedi-Soir* had fun reporting the trials and tribulations of ambassador Gay. The newspaper said that French Canada had spared no effort to come to Bernonville's defence. In its November 27 issue, *Samedi-Soir* said there was no hope left, now that France had decided not to request Bernonville's extradition. As a result, "the patronesses and vegetarians of the province of Quebec can sleep easy." Three million French Canadians could hang on to their persecuted hero.

Other newspapers, such as *L'Aurore* and *Le Populaire*, did not find the story quite so funny, and were even appalled by the attitude of Mayor Camillien Houde. The Paris daily *Le Monde* had only published a line here or that about the affair. But on November 4, it published a column signed by an expert who had lived in Canada and knew the country well. This Gaullist knew all about the depth of French-Canadian attachment to Pétain, since he had experienced it first-hand during the war, while teaching French literature at Laval University. Auguste Viatte, Marcel Trudel's former professor, was just the man to explain to French readers the events transpiring across the Atlantic.

Viatte sought first of all to explain the attitude of his French-Canadian friends. To a certain extent, he gave credence to André Laurendeau's view that this affair was a domestic quarrel. The author of the column regretted that "some agitators had gratuitously smeared France, and dragged her into their own quarrels, in order to whip up the emotions of crowds, and serve their own personal agenda." According to Viatte, that was the work of noisy Vichy supporters who had continued heaping blame on the Resistance and the Allies for their own defeat. Viatte went on to explain:

"Some of the hate-filled articles published on the shores of the St. Lawrence are every bit as bad as the worst that Berlin or Rome published during the heyday of the Axis; but they deserve only a shrug of the shoulders and it would be a mistake to believe they are anything more than the work of a small clan."

Was the former university professor thinking of Rumilly when he wrote these words? Possibly. One thing is certain: Rumilly would take it upon himself to reply in the weeks to come.

"FRANCE, AN ENORMOUS PRISON"

On November 20, 1948, exactly a month after the first declaration made by ambassador Gay, Robert Rumilly gave a speech intended as a reply to the French diplomat. At the same time, the speech was grist to the mill of Bernonville's defence. The adversaries of the former chief milicien were also Rumilly's adversaries, and were singled out for special treatment in his speech.

On that day, before the Young Chamber of Commerce of Montreal, the author of the *Histoire de la province de Québec* turned into a virulent polemicist. He started off by calling the French ambassador "a hypocritical liar". He then went on to say that "France is an enormous prison. France's entire élite is in the lockup, starting with Marshal Pétain, admirals, generals, priests, scholars, artists and writers." [11]

According to Rumilly, the purges consisted in a vast operation designed to wipe out the anti-Communist élite. "In the name of almost all of French Canada," Rumilly added, "I ask that the 40,000 Frenchmen sentenced to a slow death be amnestied." [12]

The Resistance had been made up of three sorts of Underground movements, he said. The military Underground was understandable, but then there were Communist and terrorist Underground movements as well. In fact, Rumilly said, these two last groups were blended in with the Resistance. In addition, robberies had also proliferated. So the

Resistance was made up of terrorists. One could imagine the man speaking was not Rumilly, but the Vichy's secretary of state for information, the late Philippe Henriot.

A week later, the speaker went to the palais Montcalm in Quebec City. There, before the Jeunes Laurentiens nationalist movement, he poured out all the ill will he bore towards the Resistance and the purges. He lumped Communism, terrorism and Judaism together.[13] The Red Underground, he said, had inflicted tortures "the savagery of which cannot be expressed."[14]

The speech, entitled "The truth about the Resistance and the purges in France", was quickly published in *L'Action catholique*. Philippe Hamel took care of the arrangements. He wanted to create an "atmosphere", so he decided to cover the costs of printing up and distributing the speech as a brochure. The French right-wing press repeated the gist of the speech.

The day after Rumilly's first speech in Montreal, Jean-Marie Poirier at the daily newspaper *La Presse* wrote to Rumilly. Poirier said he was neutral, that is to say neither Pétainist nor Gaullist, and was merely looking for the truth about the purges. "And it seems to me, since last Saturday, that the truth is to be found on your side."[15] Poirier concluded that "journalists always sympathize with the truth."

The former French religious Louis Even, publisher of the newspaper *Vers demain*, quickly congratulated the author "for a lecture that was both very courageous and well-documented."[16] For his part, Canon Panneton of the Monastery of the Holy Blood in Trois-Rivières, congratulated Rumilly and prayed that God bless him for his zeal in defence of the truth.[17]

Also in Trois-Rivières, another writer launched into Rumilly for attacking the Resistance. Raymond Prayal, a French resident now in Canada, reminded Rumilly that the Resistance was a national, popular movement. Rumilly was only helping the Communists in France by giving them all the credit for the struggle against the Occupation.[18]

In the November 27 issue of *Le Devoir*, the journalist Gérard Pelletier wrote sharply against Rumilly for his intentional lapses of memory. "Whatever the views of Rumilly, that great lecturer standing before Jehovah, the convenient drawers in which he stuffed the French Resistance the other evening are overflowing." Pelletier reminded Rumilly that among members of the Resistance were many Christians,

adding that "your demonstration reeks of oil and conservative prejudice."

On December 11, Eugène L'Heureux wrote in *Le Soleil* about the
"revolting lecture" given a few days previously in the Quebec capital.
"It is neither a case of a simply mistaken interpretation, nor of facts that
are hard to check, but of straight lies."

The archdiocese of Quebec was also startled by Rumilly's lecture.
The episcopate felt that this time the historian was way out of line. A
clarification had to be issued, but not because of Rumilly's words about
the Resistance and the purges. Before the Jeunes Laurentiens, Rumilly
had spoken disparagingly of the Gaullist envoy Thierry d'Argenlieu.
By association, that attack offended the memory of the recently de-
ceased Cardinal Villeneuve. In a press release, the archdiocese pointed
out that Quebec's former archbishop had maintained good relations
with General de Gaulle's envoy during the war.

On December 3, *Le Clairon* of St. Hyacinthe, which belonged to
the anticlerical Théophore-Damien Bouchard, also denounced Rumilly's lecture by publishing the words of the French journalist Jacques
Bernières who was visiting Quebec:

> "In short, and I quote: 'France is an enormous prison: were these
> suppliers of German jails the élite of France, these informers, these
> beasts of rue Lauriston and other (infamous) streets, who not only
> denounced their fellow citizens, but also had them subjected to the
> worst torture? Were these fearful and opportunistic journalists the
> élite of France, for selling their prose to the forces of Occupation?
> Were these politicians without any convictions, cravenly stooping
> before the masters of the moment, were they the élite of France? (...)
> Who are you, Sir, to sling mud in tortured faces, in your attempts to
> smear genuine heroes?"

A Canadian veteran, Major Pierre Meunier, also gave a lecture, in
which he blasted the version that Rumilly and Bernonville were spread-
ing. Since he had participated in a British mission in aid of the French
Underground, he made no bones about contradicting the two. "The
worst thing about this whole affair is not that Bernonville has found
asylum in Canada, but that it was so easy for him to find financial
backers." [19]

This point of view was not shared by the majority of people
overseas who wrote letters to Rumilly. An account of the lecture

published in the right-wing press in France and above all its distribution as a brochure widened the polemicist's readership. Philippe Hamel, Camillien Houde and Rumilly himself received hundreds of letters full of praise.

For example, on the banks of the Congo River in Brazzaville in French Equatorial Africa, a French fugitive sent his congratulations to Rumilly:

> "And it had to be in Canada, in that piece of France in America, that a strong voice made itself heard — your voice, Sir, and what a voice — to say what needed to be said about the Collaboration, the Resistance, the purges; and to smash miserable cockroaches like Francisque Gay to bits." [20]

A few months later, the same admirer wrote to Rumilly once again from Africa, and applauded his vision of French Canada:

> "We nationalists are very close to you Canadians, because you have never lost the true French spirit, and because we have found that spirit again thanks to the great master — I am referring to Charles Maurras." [21]

A letter-writer in Morocco praised the actions of Hamel and Rumilly and said he was following events closely:

> "In the eyes of our élite, French Canada is today the very picture of what our old metropolis ought to have been if she had fulfilled her vocation as the elder daughter of the Church, under the authority of our Kings (...). It is now up to you Franco-Canadians to carry the torch." [22]

A French member of the Eudist order, who was in close contact with members of his religious community established at Laval des Rapides close to Montreal, transmitted his best wishes via the community to Rumilly. On November 28, 1948, Father Jean-Baptiste Jégo wrote exactly what he thought of the new Republic from Rennes in Brittany:

> "Thank you for what you told me about Gay-the-Goatee (...). He is a sad case, like all those Zionist democrats (...). Pity the Republic. I long for its death with ever-greater fervour." [23]

Jégo would still be writing a year later, when he would castigate Gay for defending the French courts of justice. "Your Francisque has a lot of gall to go telling you good things about our Tribunals of the Liberation. They are only known by one name here: 'Courts of Injustice' ".[24]

Another French religious, Father Hervé Le Lay, of the Séminaire du St. Esprit in Chevilly-Larue, wrote in the same vein:

"Sir, continue protecting our dear brothers in French Canada from the fatal principles of the Revolution. I ardently pray for you, calling on God almighty to inspire and fortify you in the defence of Catholic, French and Latin Canada, that she may accomplish the role God confided to her in the edification of the mystical body of Jesus Christ."[25]

Another man named Reynaud wrote from Lyon where he said he was in hiding, and explained that he could give neither his address nor his first name because of "informers",[26] but vowing that Reynaud was his true name. Throughout the Bernonville affair, Reynaud would write numerous letters in defence of the count and would call on French Canadians in order to liberate Pétain. His letters all had the same bitter tone.

The range of Rumilly's partisans was large. A French journalist who said he had taken part in the Dieppe raid alongside French Canadians gave his point of view of the political aims of members in the Forces Françaises de l'Intérieur (FFI). A former member of the latter and a nationalist disciple of Maurras, Pierre-Charles Boccador of Hauteville, demanded the liberation of Pétain:

"People should know that the great majority of Real fighters, of those who painstakingly earned their stripes and a few ribbons in the FFI, were not motivated by politics but simply wanted to fight the Krauts. (...) Unfortunately, the bravest of the lot are dead. Replaced around General de Gaulle by a clique of politicians and 'Jews', political mercenaries of bankrupt parties."[27]

"A NAZI, FRENCH-SPEAKING PROVINCE: QUEBEC"

Throughout the Bernonville affair, representatives of Quebec's Jewish community followed events closely. They rarely intervened out in the open. This attitude can be attributed in large part to the fear that their public involvement in the affair would lead to a backlash in terms of immigration policy.

Irving Abella and Harold Troper have clearly shown in their ground-breaking work[28] how Canada literally closed the doors to Jewish immigration from 1938 to 1948. The year that the Bernonville affair started coincided with an easing of these restrictive policies. It was however too soon to cry victory, and the leaders of the Jewish community wanted at all costs to avoid an anti-Jewish wave.

They may have been right. On October 22, 1948, the Montreal Jewish Youth Council, an association of young Jews, protested the particular solicitude shown by the federal government in the case of the collaborators. Some of our fellow Jews, they said, were killed by these collaborators. These men should return to France to face justice.

Then, a mysterious association, the Ordre des Canadiens de naissance ("the Order of Canadians by Birth") entered the debate slamming everybody who was opposed to Bernonville, from ambassador Gay to the Canadian Legion, and the Montreal Jewish Youth Council. On October 29, *Montréal-Matin* and *La Patrie* published a shattering declaration:

"The council suggests that the payment of pensions to legionnaires be suspended for three months and that young Hebrews be deported as agents of Moscow for their disloyalty."

The hostility towards the Jewish community was shared by some official spokesmen of the pro-Bernonville movement. Rumilly was at the head of the list, along with Philippe Hamel. The Quebec dentist sought to convince a friend to join the struggle for Bernonville, by recounting all the battles he had waged up till then:

"For the last 20 years, I have been struggling without ever finding in the educated class the support that is needed to hold back that which increasingly threatens us. Just about everywhere there is a fear of displeasing the powerful or of taking them head-on. The Jewish minority, backed up by extremely active Freemasons, is less fearful and expresses its opinions openly and struggles against us in its usual shifty fashion."[29]

However, this animosity was less public than it had been before the war. During the Bernonville affair, representatives of the Canadian

Jewish Congress (CJC) did a survey of public statements. They were afraid that a fever of anti-Jewish rage like that of the 1930s could erupt again.

Statements made in the anti-Semitic magazine *L'Oeil* were also noted. The magazine (whose publication was becoming increasingly regular), blamed Bernonville's difficulties on the Communist-Jewish-Freemason triumvirate.[30]

According to the CJC representatives, the first person to start making anti-Jewish insinuations was the nationalist deputy René Chaloult. If Bernonville had been called 'Bernondsky', said Chaloult, then he would have had a much easier time staying in Canada. Jean Bonnel also said that Jews were the cause of the count's problems. However, it may be significant that the businessman subsequently denied having said as much, alleging that he had been misquoted. Finally, the anti-Semitic declarations made by Rumilly, during his lectures, were also noted.

Jewish leaders also wanted to know Jacques de Bernonville's real past. Accordingly, they contacted other organizations, such as the B'Nai Brith League in New York or well-known Jewish figures in France. André Chouraqui replied very cautiously to David Rome from Paris, saying that he had not been able to turn up much on Bernonville.

The pickings were better at the Conseil Représentatif des Juifs de France (the Jewish Representative Council of France or CRIF). The CRIF followed the affair with interest and a good deal of emotion. CRIF leaders in France brought to the attention of their fellow Jews in Canada an article which had appeared in the magazine *Action* in November 1948. They may not necessarily have written the article, but they seemed to give it credence.

The excessively provocative title of the article gives an indication of the emotions stirred on the other side of the Atlantic by the movement in Quebec to defend a collaborator: "A Nazi, French-speaking province: Quebec".[31]

"YOU ARE LISTENING TO SPANISH NATIONAL RADIO"

Farther south, in Franco's Spain, events in Quebec were viewed with satisfaction. From Barcelona where he planned to stay for awhile, Vichy's former consul general, Pierre Héricourt, paid tribute to the author of the lecture on the purges and the Resistance. In a letter dated

January 11, 1949,[32] Héricourt seized the opportunity to ask for the address of his old friend Jacques de Bernonville. He also informed Hamel and Rumilly of his intention to listen to an interesting radio talk that very evening.

A few hours after writing this letter, Héricourt plunged into the drama his compatriot was living through in Quebec. He adjusted the dial of his radio receiver and listened to a show produced by French people for French people, but broadcast from Spain. The show was conceived by Spanish National Radio and was beamed across the Pyrenees towards the population of France. This evening, however, the show spoke neither of France nor of Spain, but instead of Canada.

The host, Pierre Desjardins, described the way victims of the French purges had been welcomed on their arrival in Canada:

"Canada, like Ireland, is a country with a sense of honour and of Christian traditions of hospitality. Many French patriots hunted down because they had loyally served the legitimate government of their country, under the orders of Marshal Pétain, during the sad years of 1940-1944, have departed for Canada, where they are trying to start a new life. In general, they have been welcomed with understanding and affection by the French Canadians, who have never mistaken 'real' France for the members of a provisional Republic."[33]

Desjardins also related the struggle of Philippe Hamel and of Rumilly against ambassador Gay and quoted Hamel to the effect that "France is sick to the point of not recognizing her heroes."

On February 22, 1949, Spanish National Radio broadcast another talk on the Bernonville affair. Extracts from Rumilly's pamphlet on the purges and the Resistance were quoted. Particular reference was made to "the role and influence, at the head of the French Underground, of Red Spanish refugees in the south of France after Franco's victory..."[34]

Among former collaborators, interest in French Canada suddenly increased. Just when listeners were tuning in to Spanish National Radio, their comrades in arms in Canada were rejoicing in a new event, an event that gave them all great hope. A few hours beforehand, in Montreal, an important court decision had just been made, in favour of their compatriot Jacques de Bernonville.

FOOTNOTES

1. Letter from Julien Labedan to Robert Rumilly, September 16, 1948 (RR; ANQ; 14).

2. *The Standard*, October 16, 1948; *The Star*, October 18, 1948; *The Gazette*, October 19, 1948; *The Herald*, October 20, 1948.

3. *Le Devoir*, October 18, 1948.

4. *Le Petit Journal*, October 17, 1948. On September 12, this newspaper had published a copy of documents outlining the reasons why Paris wanted to lay its hands on Bernonville. On the anglophone side, *The Standard* had published the same information on September 11.

5. Confidential note from Camillien Houde to a senior officer of the provincial police, Fall 1948 (RR; ANQ; 14).

6. Unsigned notes (from Robert Rumilly or Jacques de Bernonville), dated October 25, 1948 (RR; ANQ; 14).

7. Letter from Jean-Marc Léger to Robert Rumilly, October 5, 1948 (RR; ANQ; 8).

8. *Montréal-Matin*, October 22, 1948.

9. Letter from Alvarez Tousignant to Francisque Gay, October 20, 1948 (RR; ANQ; 14).

10. *Le Mégantic*, November 4, 1948.

11. *Le Devoir*, November 22, 1948.

12. *Montréal-Matin*, November 22, 1948.

13. Letter from D. Kirshnblatt to Saul Hayes, December 1, 1948 (DB; ACJC).

14. Text of a speech entitled "The truth on the Resistance and the purges", by Robert Rumilly, given at the palais Montcalm before the Jeunes laurentiens, November 29, 1948 (RR; ANQ; 17).

15. Letter from Jean-Marie Poirier to Robert Rumilly, November 22, 1948 (RR; ANQ; 8).

16. Letter from Louis Even to Robert Rumilly, December 2, 1948 (RR; ANQ; 8).

17. Letter from Canon Panneton, Monastery of the Holy Blood, Trois-Rivières, to Robert Rumilly, March 19, 1949 (RR; ANQ; 17).

18. Letter from Raymond Prayal to Robert Rumilly, December 4, 1948 (RR; ANQ; 8).

19. *La Patrie*, December 7, 1948.

20. Letter from R. Pajot (Brazzaville, French Equatorial Africa) to Robert Rumilly, March 6, 1949 (RR; ANQ; 17).

21. Letter from R. Pajot (Brazzaville, French Equatorial Africa) to Robert Rumilly, July 18, 1949 (RR; ANQ; 17).

22. Letter from E. Marcy (Témara, Morocco) to Philippe Hamel, December 23, 1949 (RR; ANQ; 8).

23. Letter from Father Jean-Baptiste Jégo, a Eudist in Rennes France, to Joseph Le Lannic, a Eudist in Laval-des-Rapides, near Montreal, November 28, 1948 (RR; ANQ; 17).

24. Letter from Father Jean-Baptiste Jégo, probably to Joseph Le Lannic, December 23, 1949 (RR; ANQ; 17).

25. Letter from Hervé Le Lay, of the Séminaire du Saint-Esprit (Chevilly-Larue, France) to Robert Rumilly, July 8, 1949 (RR; ANQ; 17).

26. Letter from Reynaud, Lyon, to Camillien Houde, January 31, 1949 (RR; ANQ; 17).

27. Letter from Pierre-Charles Boccador (Hauteville, France) to Robert Rumilly, November 7, 1949 (RR; ANQ; 13).

28. Irving Abella and Harold Troper, *None is too many*, Toronto, Lester and Orpen Dennys, 1983.

29. Letter from Philippe Hamel to Dr. Pierre Jobidon, November 22, 1948 (RR; ANQ; 8).

30. Memo from D. Kishnblatt to Saul Hayes, December 8, 1948 (DB; ACJC).

31. The November 6, 1948 article in the magazine *Action* is mentioned in a memo sent by CRIF to the Canadian Jewish Congress in Montreal on May 4, 1949 (DB; ACJC).

32. Letter from Pierre Héricourt to Philippe Hamel, January 11, 1949 (RR; ANQ; 17).

33. Transcript of a Spanish National Radio talk entitled *Canada, land of independence and honour*, broadcast January 11, 1949 (RR; ANQ; 17).

34. Transcript of a Spanish National Radio talk broadcast February 22, 1949 (RR; ANQ; 17).

CHAPTER VI

Obeying a legitimate government

For some time now, Bernonville and his defenders fidgeted with impatience while awaiting the verdict of the Superior Court in Montreal. They dreaded the judgment but knew full well that it was their last hope. But then, the risk was worth it. A favourable decision would have the effect of canceling the deportation order of Immigration officials. And that would bring an end to all the worry, and mean the count and his family would be able to quietly settle in Canada.

At various times during the fall, the federal government had sent out signals to them, in order to settle out of court. Ottawa would have liked to put an end to the media campaign as quickly as possible. But Bernonville preferred to carry on with the campaign, in the hopes of setting a precedent for other Frenchmen facing the same problems.

On February 21, 1949, Justice Louis Cousineau delivered his verdict. He said that the deportation order was illegal. And he went even further. He cleared Bernonville of any blame for his past. In his judgment, Cousineau noted the sudden disappearance of the Vichy régime at the end of the war, without any further comment:

> "His testimony indicates clearly first of all that he always behaved in an irreproachable fashion and that he fled his country because, having fulfilled his role at the request of the legitimate government of France, he was being hunted and tracked down and faced mortal danger after the disappearance of the government of Marshal Pétain, (a government duly recognized by Canada) and after the Marshal

himself was imprisoned. It is therefore clear that Bernonville was a political exile when he arrived in Canada." [1]

Justice Cousineau was not particularly upset about Count de Bernonville's illegal entry into Canada using forged papers. On several occasions, he said, Canada admitted people into the country without asking to see their papers. He was thinking especially of people having fled the Soviet régime.

If Great Britain had been placed in the same position as Canada, she would certainly have granted asylum to Bernonville. Over the centuries, Great Britain had been a land of refuge for many exiles, among them Catholic priests having escaped the French Revolution. That was a historical fact.

Bernonville and his family were exultant. He immediately scribbled a note of thanks to one of his most powerful protectors, Camillien Houde. The same day, he received journalists in his Montreal home, at 5551 Côte des Neiges, at the foot of St. Joseph's Oratory. Free French veterans hard on his heels called the place "Au Petit Pétain". [2]

This time round, Jacques de Bernonville could break the silence imposed on him by the never-ending discussions during his trial. He detailed the reasons he had come to Canada, under the anxious gaze of his wife, who clearly wanted to end the discussion as quickly as possible. He had fought for order all his life. Canada happened to share his social ideas. Besides:

> "When I left France, I had the choice of four or five countries I could have gone to knowing that I would obtain justice. I wanted to choose Canada because I believe it is a free and democratic country with a Christian tradition...." [3]

The woes of France, he continued, were essentially due to the fact that people had disobeyed authority too much.

The day had begun with the victory of the judgment and the litany of confidences Bernonville poured out to journalists. But it did not end the same way. Bernonville's Canadian plans collapsed once again. In the federal Parliament, MacKinnon, the minister responsible for immigration, dismissed the verdict delivered earlier in the day in Montreal. He announced that a second board of inquiry would be set up to re-examine Jacques de Bernonville's case.

The following day, newspapers that had been hostile to Bernonville did not know whether to react with shock or joy to the confusing turn of events. The Montreal newspaper *The Herald* praised the minister's decision to open up the Bernonville affair again. *The Gazette* concentrated instead on the judgment made by Cousineau, who had clearly overstepped his mandate. It was not up to the judge to determine whether Bernonville could be categorized as a political refugee. But that was what the judge had done.

The newspaper *Le Canada* meanwhile was still reeling under the shock of Cousineau's verdict, which it considered revolting. According to Rageur, the editorial-writer of the Liberal newspaper, the real winners of the trial were:

> "(...) the shifty-eyed wogs who dared say that 'France was an enormous prison' (...) The wretched scum of the Kollaboration, fugitives in the lands of Franco and of Peron, have triumphed.
>
> (...) In the extrajudicial unraveling of the entire affair is a deliberate sabotage of our war aims, of our democratic principles, of our alliances with great nations." [4]

At first, the federal government's attitude seemed astonishing. A decision now gave it the chance to bury an affair that was hurting national unity - and suddenly the government was the first to start up the whole story all over again.

In the inner circle of the government in Ottawa, people knew only too well what was at stake. Louis St. Laurent had been the official head of government since November 15, 1948, and he quickly grasped the fact that Canadian electors had diametrically opposed expectations in this debate. He had only just come into office, and was now faced with a tug-of-war.

Since the fall, letters from many English Canadian associations poured into his office. They all protested against the way the government had acted in the case of the presumed collaborators. Most of the letters demanded their deportation.

In the front ranks of these demands one finds the Loyal Orange Association, Province of Ontario. Without a doubt, sheer hostility to French Canadians now found an acceptable outlet and could be openly expressed with a clear conscience. But the Orangemen's letter does not faithfully represent the majority of letters sent to St. Laurent, which were mainly from appalled Anglican ministers, veterans' associations in Ontario asking that justice be done, shocked Manitoban academics, charitable and human rights associations and Jewish organizations, all of them venting their indignation at the fact the Canadian government had chosen to ignore what the French fugitives had done.

The letters sent to St. Laurent by French Canadians were of a completely different nature. For example, Conrad Bérubé, an ardent supporter of the mayor of Montreal, wrote:

"I would much rather see people of Mr. de Bernonville's quality than all sorts of immigrants that Canada takes in every month and who come here to take our places of honour - and we Canadians, who are Canadians and not Jews and Communists, we want a healthy and honest immigration."[5]

St. Laurent was thus aware of the deep division that could result from this affair. Personally, he had no particular opinions about the past actions of the Frenchmen. Given the context at the time, that was not too surprising. After 1945, the question of war criminals had quickly fallen by the wayside, in Canada and in other countries.

On July 13, 1948, the British sent a secret telegram to Canada and to six other former colonies of the Empire. London suggested it was just as well to stop investigations that had been started to hunt down presumed war criminals. Canada acknowledged receipt of the telegram, but only said it had taken note of the suggestion. In the 30 years to come, Canada developed an attitude of laisser-faire and extradition requests, mainly from countries in Eastern Europe, were rejected.

The official opposition shared the views of the government on this question. Indeed, the Progressive Conservative Party, led by George Drew, had many reasons to stay silent. Its avowed anti-Communism kept it from jumping into the fray against Bernonville. But there was something else. On January 26, 1949, the well-known Montreal botanist Jacques Rousseau delivered a warning to the party. To a senior member of the Conservative Party Rousseau gave this advice:

"It is important that the Conservatives not ask questions in the House. I am sure that if questions were allowed to be raised about Mr. de Bernonville, this would definitely serve the interests of French Communists."[6]

Rousseau warned that a declaration made by the Conservatives could be a fatal blow to their chances of gaining votes in Quebec. The message was received loud and clear - and Drew gave the order that nothing should be said on the subject. The only Conservative to speak out about the collaborators was John Diefenbaker, who later accused the government of having secretly adopted ministerial orders on behalf of the four Frenchmen. However, Diefenbaker did not say a word about Bernonville.

The Liberal Party had nothing to worry about in the case of the Conservatives. The CCF, a party at the cross-section of several political traditions, was another story altogether. The CCF was at the meeting-point of the labour brand of socialism, populism and social democracy. Allister Stewart, the CCF MP for the Manitoba riding of Winnipeg North, began a one-man combat against the French collaborators who had found refuge in Canada.[7] In his parliamentary campaign, he had the support of two allies: the English-language press and particularly *The Globe & Mail*, and veterans of the Free French forces settled in Montreal.

Michel Pichard, a decorated veteran of the Resistance, led this latter group. He took over from Jokelson, the man who had discovered Bernonville's presence in Canada in the first place. Along with his friends, Pichard constituted a Canadian beach-head for fellow veterans in France who wanted Bernonville to face justice. Starting in Fall 1948, he began to transmit information between various French veterans associations and the MP Stewart. One of his contacts in France was none other than Colonel Romans-Petit, who knew Bernonville very well. At the beginning of 1944, in Upper Savoy, Romans-Petit had sent Lieutenant Tom Morel to occupy the heights of Glières. Morel was never to return. The troops commanded by Bernonville trapped many of Morel's companions in the Maquis.

At the beginning of 1949, Stewart obtained some extremely compromising information about Bernonville. It consisted of the testimony of the victims of crimes committed by Bernonville and his troops during the Occupation. The information had been sent along by French veterans.

St. Laurent knew that Stewart had this information and that he would make it public in the event that a judgment came down in Bernonville's favour. That is why St. Laurent decided to catch the CCF deputy unawares, and announce that he planned to launch a second inquiry into the French fugitives.

TESTIMONY OF A BUCHENWALD SURVIVOR

The order given to the bureaucrats to begin new proceedings against Bernonville did not deter Stewart. The very next day, the MP for Winnipeg North decided to rise in the House, in order to pressure the bureaucrats to get their inquiry under way as fast as possible.

On February 22, Stewart rose and made disturbing revelations about Bernonville's past. For the most part these revelations consisted in testimonies collected together and mailed to Michel Pichard by Colonel Romans-Petit, director of the Fédération Nationale du Maquis. Evidence provided by the garage mechanic Maurice Nedey was particularly moving.

On June 20, 1944, Nedey was captured by a Milice unit in the region of Saône-et-Loire, then led to the Hôtel Moderne in Chalon-sur-Saône. The following day, June 21, Commander de Bernonville came to the hotel, which had been transformed into his headquarters, and was informed of the capture. Maurice Nedey was then led to a large room where he was undressed. The room was then emptied, leaving only a desk, behind which Bernonville sat. The interrogation could begin. Here is the testimony, as reported by Stewart:

"De Bernonville, seated behind his desk, did not sully or tire himself to torture me; he merely gave the orders and led the course of interrogation. These orders were as follows: 'Question him', 'make him talk', 'talk', 'stop', 'continue', 'it's to your interest to talk and tell us all', 'I am in a hurry and have no time to waste'. All the staff I mentioned above rivaled each other in cruelty. They spat on me, hit me with their fists, kicked me in the stomach. I warded off the blows as much as I could but one of them lashed me with a whip across the stomach and I thought I would vomit out my guts. I dropped to the floor time after time but they immediately made me get on my feet again by kicking me in the sides. They stood in a circle and pushed me from one to the other. I began to realize I could not stand this for long. Then I got a tremendous blow which broke my lower jaw and I spat out bits of teeth broken by the shock." [8]

Bernonville then asked where the weapons were stashed, demanding to know the names of other members of the Underground, the passwords for different parachute-drops, the location of radio transmitters, the places where British airmen were hidden.

When Bernonville got nowhere with this interrogation, he ordered torture with electricity. Nedey felt as if a knife-blade were turning in his chest, right next to his heart. He screamed, choked. At regular intervals, the Miliciens stopped and then started again.

Nedey pointed out that Bernonville was impassive. The mechanic pleaded with him and then finally accepted to sign a confession that he didn't read. Throughout the night, Bernonville continued accusing him of being a traitor and insisting that it was a disgrace to work for England, since honour required that he serve Marshal Pétain.

On June 22, despite Commander de Bernonville's assurances, a voice shrieked at the door of the cell. It was the Gestapo, waiting for the Miliciens to hand over their prisoner. Nedey was deported to Buchenwald, where he managed to survive.

Stewart did not stop there. He also explained Bernonville's activities in North Africa and his role in France hunting down members of the Resistance. He related Bernonville's work in identifying British officers parachuted into France.

Once Stewart had exposed the gruesome details of Bernonville's past, he turned to the other French fugitives who had found refuge in Canada. He denounced Dr. Georges Benoit Montel, Dr. André Boussat, Julien Labedan and Jean Louis Huc. Then came startling news. Stewart revealed the presence in Canada of a sixth French collaborator, a 42-year-old physician, Dr. Michel Seigneur, who had served in the Milice and had been convicted by a court in Poitiers. Stewart said:

> "I know the department cannot possibly keep watch at every point on the border, but there are some of these people in this country, and they have been smuggled in. It is time the country knew how this is done." [9]

The following day, the Montreal daily *The Herald* devoted its front page to the testimony of Maurice Nedey. The entire first page of the newspaper was filled with the Allister Stewart's statements. The French-Canadian press also featured them prominently. However, most newspapers reported Stewart's words in haste, without giving them any particular credit. On February 23, a headline in *Le Devoir* read "A socialist deputy attacks the French political refugees". On another page,

Pierre Vigeant interpreted Allister Stewart's statements as an attack on all immigration that was French or likely to speak French.

Roger Duhamel, the publisher of *Montréal-Matin*, was not impressed by the documents incriminating Bernonville. On that day, he wrote:

> "What have they changed? How many times do we have to repeat, to the chagrin of our servile compatriots who are jockeying for the Légion d'honneur, that we object to every judgment made by the revolutionary tribunals created after the dreadful liberation?"

During the affair, Duhamel challenged any and all accusations, by seizing on unfounded declarations about Bernonville's past published by newspapers opposing him. For example, some newspapers gave 1898 as Bernonville's year of birth, rather than 1897. Duhamel used such examples to undermine the newspaper attacks on Bernonville.

On February 23, an unidentified member of the committee for his defence telephoned Bernonville, asking him to rush out and get a copy of the *Herald*. The newspaper contained extremely embarrassing statements made by Stewart, which could make Bernonville's defence more difficult.

Bernonville picked up the newspaper and read the accusations made against him. The former chief Milicien set to work, refuting point by point the assertions made by the CCF deputy. That same day, he contacted his protector to explain the substance of his defence. First of all, he was not in Chalon-sur-Saône during the period described by Maurice Nedey. Second, he had never collaborated with the Nazis. And third, he had never set foot in Tunisia. Bernonville concluded by stating that in Spring 1944, he had not been named military governor of Lyon by the Gestapo, but by Marshal Pétain instead.

As for Robert Rumilly, he swiftly wrote to the French right-wing weekly *Aspects de la France*, in order to obtain information about Maurice Nedey and eventually link him to the Communists. At the same time, he requested other documents and explained that:

> "A list of priests who were massacred, convicted or are currently in prison would be an extremely useful document." [10]

The next day, February 24, one of Bernonville's protectors came to his rescue in the House of Commons. The independent member for

Charlevoix-Saguenay, Frédéric Dorion, rose in the House on Bernon-ville's behalf. He made such a strong speech that the leaders of the Ecole sociale populaire decided to publish it as a brochure.

Dorion's strategy was to reply to Stewart's evidence with the well-oiled arguments of the count's defenders in Quebec. He made the following statement:

> "I am sure that if the French citizens that the member for Winnipeg North has spoken about had been Communist Jews instead of French Catholics, we would not have heard about them." [11]

In the Commons, the CCF members were increasingly uneasy, and their leader called out "shame, shame" while Dorion spoke. The member for Saguenay brought up some of the usual themes in his defence of the fugitive. He said that the Resistance was almost entirely made up of Communists; he said that France's justice system was inadequate. And he repeated that Bernonville had only been following the orders of the legitimate government of Marshal Pétain.

If anyone had ever deserved the right to asylum in Canada, Dorion continued, it was this man victimized by Communist persecution. Dorion said that:

> "This question is much more important than the fate of a few individuals. The principle at stake is the struggle between Commu-nists and Christianity." [12]

A few days later, *The Standard* of Montreal published the words of Bernonville's arch-enemy, Colonel Romans-Petit. The revelations had first appeared in *Voix du Maquis*, the official organ of veterans of the French Resistance. In his open letter, Romans-Petit accused Ber-nonville of being among the great leaders who had betrayed the interests of France during the Nazi Occupation. "We were more afraid of the Milice than we were of the Nazis," said the colonel.

Free French veterans in Montreal were determined to explain to French Canadians what the Milice had really been like. In general, these Frenchmen wrote to *Le Canada* under a single name: Jean Bourgetel. The latter name had been chosen since Bourgetel was the only one among them to have Canadian citizenship.

Bourgetel had served in the air force during the war. On March 11, he related his experience with the Milice after landing by parachute in Brittany on the night of June 5-6, 1944:

"These men were fearsome and more cruel than the most brutal German SS." [13]

He said that it was impossible that Bernonville didn't know about the tortures inflicted by some Miliciens on members of the Resistance. He said that given Bernonville's high position, he had to know about the use of cold baths, electric current, burning with cigars, beating with rifle butts and riding whips.

Bourgetele detected in this collaborator a born manipulator:

"You are a hypocrite because today, knowing that you are in a very Catholic province, you are trying to replace the swastika, under which you served not long ago, with the cross of Christ, in order to obtain the protection of some influential people, and by using the most common slogan people use these days in self-defence: 'I am an anti-Communist'". [14]

When this open letter was written, the second committee of inquiry into Jacques de Bernonville's past had not yet begun its work. The minister responsible for the committee even assured a Quebec MP, Wilfrid Lacroix, that he was going to slow things down. In any case, federal elections were fast approaching.

Envoys from the federal government concluded a tacit agreement with the count's defenders to get them to stop making so many waves. Camillien Houde, Robert Rumilly and the others agreed not to talk about it any more. Bernonville was encouraged to distance himself from his protectors. The federal envoys suggested to him that the matter could end up dying on the order-paper.

However, at the very same moment, a secret telegram from the Canadian ambassador in Paris to Prime Minister St. Laurent left little doubt about the federal government's real intentions. On March 12, 1949, Georges Vanier outlined the steps he had taken with the French authorities. [15]

First of all, Vanier summarized the government's strategy. Up till now, he said, the position of the federal government had been dictated by the need to keep well away from the political debate. On technical grounds, illegal entry into the country was sufficient grounds to justify deportation.

Between the lines, Vanier suggested a new approach. The government should make its next move on the grounds of treason. The ambassador said he had consulted French officials about the release of compromising documents about Bernonville. He concluded that the officials would have no objection.

The affair now entered a stagnant phase that was neither joyful nor worrisome. Some people, such as Victor Keyserling, had a realistic idea of the forces at play. After working for the Vichy broadcaster Radio-Paris during the Occupation. Keyserling had fled to Canada after the war with his real identity papers. Once he got to Montreal, he began work for British United Press. But his application for a permanent residence permit ran into a roadblock when federal officials launched an inquiry. Rumilly was sympathetic but said he could do little to help. In any case, Keyserling had no intention of raising a political storm. He would rather leave than see a single line in print about his case. Just before immigration authorities were due to render their decision, Keyserling was already planning a way out;

"(...) it is too hard to take on the whole administration of the government. It is far better to leave like a gentleman than to become a football field for politicians in search of electoral arguments." [16]

Shortly afterward, Victor Keyserling and his family left Canada for Haiti.

As for Bernonville, he had a series of jobs in Montreal while waiting for events to unfold. Things were looking up. In Summer 1949, the committee set up to study his case had not yet met. Rumilly followed events from his residence in the Town of Mount Royal, ready to set off the alarm if need be. In mid-August, he detected some activity in Ottawa. He contacted the editorial-writer André Laurendeau, who reassured him. Nevertheless, Laurendeau informed him that a commentary had come out that very day "reminding the government to be sensible".[17]

On August 19, Laurendeau wrote a brief commentary in Le Devoir hoping that the new committee never saw the light of day. He wrote that:

"Count de Bernonville was a political refugee, and has the right to the same welcome in this country as the refugees of all races that are allowed in to Canada. The right to asylum is just as urgent for us when a French citizen is involved."

But news was no longer so reassuring. During the same period, Rumilly heard some parliamentary gossip which struck him as very threatening. The recent federal election had returned Louis St. Laurent's Liberals to power. During the holidays, the wife of the prime minister had supposedly said:

"De Bernonville will be deported. My husband will not risk a diplomatic incident for him." [18]

A QUESTION OF IDENTITY

In January 1950, it was an inescapable fact that the federal government was getting ready to re-open the file. The inquiry had finally been set in motion. On February 16, 1950, immigration authorities officially announced their intention of deporting Bernonville.

The dormant forces around Rumilly shook themselves awake at the beginning of the year. The first step was to obtain the services of a first-class nit-picker in order to exhaust all legal recourse. The lawyer Bernard Bourdon accepted Edouard Masson's help in this respect. Ultimately, they did extremely well, although their first steps were faltering. One of their lawyers left them in the lurch at the outset. Roger Ouimet was distressed by what he learned and feared that the affair would become a hot media issue once more. On January 27, he wrote to Bernonville:

"The closer the deadline gets, the more I realize that this affair goes well beyond individual people and in spite of you is becoming a political affair. I realize I cannot do anything for you. I regret that I did not know as much as I now know before accepting to take up your case." [19]

The Committee for the Defence of French Political Refugees got back to work. It planned to mobilize public opinion. The strategy consisted in soliciting the help of French-Canadian organizations, which were encouraged to send letters, telegrams, resolutions or petitions to Ottawa.

Rumilly and his friends also banked on French-Canadian parliamentarians. The historian informed his friend Chaloult of the presence in Ottawa of a Liberal MP highly sympathetic to the Bernonville family. The MP was highly indignant about the fact that proceedings against Bernonville had got underway again; even though the MP sat on the government benches, he planned to help Bernonville. According to him, several French-Canadian MPs in his own party were of the same view.

Meanwhile, on February 21, the Liberal MP for Témiscouata, Jean-François Pouliot, announced to the press that he also sympathized with Bernonville. He even proposed that the latter be named French ambassador in Ottawa. Following the precedent set by Dorion, who had been defeated in the last federal election, Pouliot declared that the accusation against Bernonville was without any foundation. The accusation had been produced by a justice system in the clutches of the Communists. Almost exactly one year after Frédéric Dorion had spoken in the House, Pouliot took up Dorion's theme:

"(...) if the latter had been a Freemason, nobody would have objected to his remaining in the country." [20]

On March 3, 1950, a heavyweight Liberal MP rose to defend Count de Bernonville. The MP for Bonaventure, Bona Arsenault, spoke in the presence of his nervous anglophone colleagues:

"Convinced as I am of the innocence and the perfect worthiness of Count de Bernonville, I believe it is my duty, despite all the drawbacks my attitude might create, to make my voice heard in this House, in favour of a French citizen who is persecuted by his political enemies, persecuted by French Communist organizations, and persecuted here by their notorious sympathizers." [21]

Arsenault followed in the footsteps of his predecessors. The attacks against Bernonville were a tissue of lies. Accusations made by Communist purge trials could not be taken seriously.

Philippe Hamel rejoiced in Bona Arsenault's speech and immediately offered his congratulations to Rumilly. "This clear and well-documented exposé sounds like it could be your prose." [22] Rumilly spoke out as well, but in a way that was far more virulent and damaging for the party in power. Liberal MPs who supported Bernonville's cause were so embarrassed by Rumilly's words, that they told him to calm down. Jean-François Pouliot issued a stern warning:

"If you really want to help Bernonville, you are better off finding a more appropriate tone than you usually have in your lectures, or not speaking at all." [23]

Five days after Bona Arsenault's speech, an Opposition MP showed his colours. Henri Courtemanche, Conservative MP for Labelle, was the first Opposition MP to speak up for Bernonville in the federal Parliament.

As a whole, French-Canadian members were rather sympathetic to Bernonville but did not go as far as Pouliot, Arsenault and Courtemanche. Rumilly's pressures tactics, by claiming that Bernonville was "a victim of Communists and Judeo-Freemasons" had little effect.[24] But some MPs participated in less compromising ways.

An internal opinion poll conducted on Parliament Hill by an independent firm revealed that Bernonville had a lot of support among French-Canadian MPs. This *vox populi* was without scientific merit, but indicated that 38 French-speaking MPs out of 40 were favourably disposed toward Bernonville. However, support in the House did not just come from French Canadians alone. A single English-speaking MP broke the law of silence and offered his support to Bernonville.

Meanwhile, Anatole and Guy Vanier worked assiduously so that telegrammes and letters flooded in to ministers' offices from all directions. On March 13, Anatole Vanier explained to Émilien Rochette of Charlesbourg in the Quebec City suburbs, the reasons for doing this:

"We have to support this French Catholic, whom the bureaucracy in Ottawa want to sacrifice, after letting in all kinds of strangers without any identification from all over Central Europe, and where the Jewish element must have predominated without anyone noticing." [25]

While Rumilly worked at getting people to write letters to the editor of different newspapers, the Vaniers worked across the province in drawing up resolutions. The Société St. Jean Baptiste of Montreal, the Chicoutimi Chamber of Commerce, the City Council of Rouyn sent their pleas to the minister of Immigration. The letters all demanded that Count de Bernonville, a political refugee, be granted asylum.

The Société St. Jean Baptiste of Montreal urged Prime Minister St. Laurent to be lenient, and drew a parallel with some Patriotes after the 1837-38 Rebellion, who were granted asylum abroad. Barrière, the first person to organize a petition-signing campaign in Bernonville's defence laid plans for a march of 500 people to Ottawa to demand an order-in-council for Bernonville. But the demonstration never took place.

J.-A. Mongrain, the mayor of Trois-Rivières, joined the fray. On March 30, 1950, a letter he had sent to St. Laurent appeared in the press. The letter contained a veiled threat about the Liberals ("les Rouges" or the Reds in common Quebec parlance):

"If it turns out this request is ignored, and people insist on deporting the Count, I have the impression that a great many of our French Canadian fellow citizens would see red because of an act bordering on barbarity..." [26]

The nationalist movement of the Jeunesses patriotes du Canada français sent a devastating letter to Walter Harris, the minister of Immigration and Citizenship. The letter's authors, Walter O'Leary, André Mathieu and René Sarrasin laid out on the table the all-important question of immigration:

"Fortunately, Count de Bernonville's case demonstrates to our people all the danger of having the political control of a racist immigration in the hands of the Anglo-Canadian majority." [27]

Then the young nationalists issued the minister a sharp warning:

"We demand the control of our immigration because we are directly threatened in our French lifestyle by the increasingly invasive anglophone floodtide. We want to choose our immigrants the way you choose yours, but we will base our choice on our culture and not on their race the way you have done too often.

"And only then will we be able to legally make of a man like Count de Bernonville a French-Canadian citizen, as you have so often done with so many Anglo-Canadian citizens under the label of 'Canadian'".

On February 28, 1950, *Montréal-Matin* developed similar points. The newspaper had a hard time understanding why the Canadian government was so obstinate in Bernonville's case. The writer was clearly frustrated, and pleaded that immigration rules be applied rigorously. Given the context of the time, it is hard not to see that the foreigners referred to by the newspaper were representatives of the Jewish minority:

> "We ask the minister of Immigration to carefully examine his files and to tell us whether other foreigners might possibly have entered Canada in the same conditions as Count de Bernonville and have not had to take the grueling punishment that has been inflicted on him and on his family over close to two years."

When the struggle pitting the federal government against Bernonville broke out again, *Le Devoir* published a new commentary. On February 24, under the heading "Bloc-Notes", Paul Sauriol pointed out that the British government had taken a new position in comparable cases. Indeed, Great Britain had recently decided to grant asylum to former criminals pursued by Allied countries as war criminals. The question whether an individual was a war criminal or not was of secondary importance, the newspaper said:

> "Quite apart from the accusations made against him in France, shouldn't we imitate England's behavior?"

In any case, said the columnist, the acts he was accused of in France were not common-law offences.

He then took up the themes that had already been used in defence of the count, among them the partiality of the courts:

> "(...) French prisons hold many convicts who are only there on account of their political opinions and actions, and for which a large part of French public opinion demands an amnesty."

Le Canada let the veterans speak in the new phase of its campaign against Bernonville. The newspaper seemed less cocky after losing its editor-in-chief, Guy Jasmin, who had been killed in an air crash in the Azores, along with the French boxer Marcel Cerdan.

On March 27, the newspaper published a letter that had been sent by the Association du Corps Canadien du Québec to Louis St. Laurent.

The spokesman, Roméo Tanguay, refuted the parallel drawn with the Patriotes, and asked the government to do its duty and send Jacques de Bernonville back to France to face judgment. Tanguay was particularly angry with the count's defenders, who were the same people to have opposed Canada's active military participation during the war.

The English-language press, meanwhile, with some nuances here and there, still unanimously demanded the count's deportation. That was just as true of the *Winnipeg Free Press* as of *The Ottawa Citizen*. Only a few anglophone religious periodicals came out in support of Bernonville.

At this point, it seemed the affair could swing in the count's favour just as much as toward straight deportation. The pro-Bernonville camp was determined to get asylum for him, and therefore planned a big move in Spring 1950. It would appeal to the French-Canadian intelligentsia and all the best-known and most credible people in the province. The objective was to bring together as many of these names as possible on a petition and to send it to Ottawa, demanding asylum for Bernonville. His supporters were convinced that a request coming from the élite of French Canada would create a huge impression and would bring an end to the affair.

Rumilly and others busily knocked on doors. Some people were reticent but polite, some refused to compromise themselves. The historian Guy Frégault, author of *La civilisation de la Nouvelle-France*, diplomatically declined the invitation. On April 14, he wrote to Rumilly:

"To my great regret, I must abstain from signing the petition which you have kindly sent me. I feel honoured by the confidence you have shown, but I know too little about the Bernonville affair to be able to intervene." [28]

Adrien Pouliot, the Dean of Science at Laval University, sent a similar answer to Rumilly. While he was "very sympathetic to Commander de Bernonville",[29] the scientist indicated that he disliked signing mass petitions. He much preferred sending a letter along to the deputy minister of Immigration in order to receive an explanation of the affair. In fact, Pouliot's attitude toward Bernonville was not very sympathetic at all.

On the other hand, other members of the élite answered the appeal with enthusiasm. The committee obtained the signatures of 143 people, all of them well-known in their respective fields. The April 17, 1950 petition was sent to Walter Harris, the minister responsible for Immigration in Ottawa. It demanded that the decision taken by the committee of inquiry into Count de Bernonville be reversed. It said the issues were the humanity and the reputation of Canada.

Among those who signed were many noteworthy people: doctors, lawyers and notaries. The names of bankers, well-known academics and priests appeared side by side. The leaders of nationalist organizations were almost all on the list. The petition included: Arthur Tremblay, president of the Société St. Jean Baptiste of Montreal; Éva Rodier-Thibodeau, president of the Fédération nationale St. Jean Baptiste; Guy Marcotte, president of the Association canadienne des jeunesses catholiques; Anatole Vanier, president of the Ligue nationale; Léo Guindon, president of the Alliance nationale des professeurs catholiques de Montréal; André Mathieu, president of the Jeunesses patriotes; et Rosaire Morin, president-general of the Jeunesses laurentiennes.

There was a strong contingent at the Université de Montréal: Mgr. Olivier Maurault, rector; Édouard Montpetit, secretary-general; Canon Arthur Sideleau, dean of Arts and his secretary Jean Houpert; Guy Vanier of the faculty of social, economic and political sciences.

Also on the petition were: Pierre Dagenais, director of the Institut de géographie; Maxime Raymond, former federal leader of the Bloc Populaire; Victor Barbeau of the Académie canadienne-française; Jacques rousseau, director of the Montreal Botanical Gardens; Léopold Richer of the Académie and publisher of the newspaper *Notre temps*. A young psychiatrist, many years later the Parti québécois minister who introduced Quebec's controversial language law (Bill 101), Dr. Camille Laurin, also signed the petition.[30]

Two weeks later, Bernonville warmly thanked those who had signed the petition:

"The communion of ideas and tradition which I feel so keenly between Canadians and myself has just been strengthened..."[31]

RÉMY, ISORNI OR WEYGAND?

The community of ideas of which Bernonville spoke did not offer much in the way of concrete political benefits, according to his organizers. In other words, they felt the best way to make the Bernonville campaign effective was to integrate it into one of the country's great political causes.

One example illustrates the mentality prevailing among some French-Canadian intellectuals. When Rumilly sought to gain the support of his friend Léopold Richer, he pointed out to him one day the partisan line that their common adversaries took on the Resistance. Since their adversaries had supported the Resistance, it made sense to take the opposite view.

Anatole Vanier wrote to Prime Minister St. Laurent about Vichy on June 8, 1950:

"Can we really believe (...) that Ottawa's point of view is necessarily the same as Quebec's in the international domain?"[32]

It is worth going more deeply into the question of partisan lines. At the Committee for the Defence of French Political Refugees, organizers thought it was time to launch a vast public information campaign. Exploiting alliances would help channel greater energies in favour of the count. And by the same token that would strengthen the political convictions of the public. The organizers considered that there was a deplorable amount of confusion on this score among French Canadians and that lessened the intensity of their commitment.

Once Houde, Hamel and Rumilly dug through the mountain of letters they had received, they naturally concluded that some prominent figures in France would be good at enlightening the people of Quebec. Anatole Vanier believed there was already a bridge of solidarity linking New France "and the best elements of Old France".[33] The current struggle over Count de Bernonville represented in his view a fight to the death between Left and Right. An appeal to the traditional French Right could help strengthen sympathies which otherwise might wane.

Contacts were established. Commander Quivaux, who remained loyal to the Marshal, quickly let Mayor Houde understand the breadth of support that could be obtained in France. Quivaux wanted the favour to be returned:

"I think that if three million French Canadian out of the three and a half million living in Canada signed petitions sent to the president of the French Republic, as brothers by race and conviction, such a tremendous gesture on the part of Canada would not leave the current masters of the destiny of France indifferent and would help to liberate the 40,000 who suffer and die each day in prison for having recognized Marshal Pétain as the legal head of France." [34]

The committee was very busy and did not follow up on the request made by Quivaux. But contacts continued. Abel Bonnard, Vichy's former minister of National Education and a comrade of Bernonville's, showed signs of life. He was now a refugee in Spain. But he did no more than make a show of solidarity. "He is a soldier, he is a gentleman, he is a knight." [35] Jean Tracou, Pétain's former chief of staff, responded in much the same way. He confirmed the relationship existing between Pétain and Bernonville.

While studying in Paris at the beginning of 1950, Jean-Marc Léger offered to accomplish various tasks for the count in the French capital. He remained sympathetic to Bernonville and his family, and had a student bursary enabling him to study at an institute of political studies and at a law faculty. On January 24, 1950, Léger wrote to Rumilly:

> "If by my presence in Paris I were able to serve some useful purpose in this affair, take various measures, etc., it would be with the greatest pleasure that I would endeavour to help in some way a family for which I conserve such deep respect and such warm sympathy." [36]

In reply to this offer, Rumilly asked him simply to let all his acquaintances know that:

> "the French government will hurt its own image among French Canadians by persecuting Commander de Bernonville and by insisting on his deportation." [37]

Contact was finally established by people in Montreal and Jacques Isorni, the lawyer who had defended Pétain and Robert Brasillach. Rumilly got to know him at the time he had been considering writing a biography of the Marshal. Isorni was chosen by the committee to represent Bernonville's interest in France. The lawyer said he was honoured to be chosen.

Jacques Isorni had good press in all Catholic and nationalist newspapers in the province. *Le Devoir* published an article by the French jurist on February 8, 1950, underlining the importance and the value of this statement, given "the remarkable competence" of its author.

Isorni had been approached at first for something else. Some organizers had thought of inviting him to Canada in order to reply in person to ambassador Francisque Gay. The idea was dropped, whether because he had divorced or for some other reason. So the committee's initial idea of informing and rehabilitating Pétain in the eyes of French Canadians, took some time to ripen.

Meanwhile, Philippe Hamel raged against French-Canadian newspapers for being increasingly favourable to General de Gaulle. Hamel's friend, Maxime Weygand, shared this revulsion for de Gaulle. He said to him:

> "I do not understand why General de Gaulle still has admirers in your country." [38]

Hamel finally decided to take on the Gaullists of Quebec himself. This nationalist waited awhile for the Quebec government to provide some financial support to bring lecturers over from France, but the idea seemed to have got bogged down.

In Summer 1950, a controversy raged between Hamel and Marthe Simard. A decorated veteran of the French Resistance, Simard dealt a blistering attack on Hamel for disparaging de Gaulle. On July 27, 1950, *L'Action catholique* published her open letter. She was outraged and noted that Hamel did not seem to care much about Canada's military involvement in the last war.

> "Dr. Philippe Hamel seems to forget that Canada was at war with Germany, just like Free France under the orders of General de Gaulle (...)
>
> As for the people who have been 'purged' - which you claim is the shame of the Liberation - forget them in the slime where they are stuck and dying. And think about the French men and women, both young and old, who were their victims in flesh and spirit."

The exchange soon died down, leaving Hamel feeling hurt. He was sure the press were preventing him from getting his good name back. He felt that the religious hierarchy, by hesitating and even expressing disapproval, had showed a lack of courage.

Rumilly got the dentist thinking again about the idea of inviting a French lecturer. He spoke to him of a certain Colonel Rémy. Gilbert Renault, alias Colonel Rémy, was a hero of the Resistance, and had published his war memoirs under the title *Mémoires d'un agent secret de la France libre*. On April 11, 1950, he published a long article that revived the thesis that Pétain had been 'the shield' enabling de Gaulle 'the sword' to find room to attack. Two weeks later, he quit the Rassemblement du Peuple Français.

This was the backdrop for the negotiations that got underway between Rémy and Vichy supporters in Quebec who were inviting him to Canada. While Guy Vanier was in Europe, he met Jacques Isorni, and almost went to see Rémy. Vanier and Rémy agreed on the idea, and Vanier asked that he continue discussions with Rumilly.

On August 6, Rémy wrote to Rumilly. The documents that had been published since the Liberation made him reconsider his judgment of Marshal Pétain. Then Rémy got to the point. Guy Vanier had explained the interest of coming to Canada to give a few lectures. He liked the idea.

"I would gladly come to Canada, at a date to be arranged later, if you thought that in your country it could usefully serve a cause whose victory must mean the triumph of truth and justice, at the same time as it would help bring about the reconciliation of the French people - in the best sense."[39]

One wonders how much Rémy knew about the affair then underway in Canada. In his letter to Rumilly, he seemed to want to explain his new position on Pétain to French Canadians. He also clearly wanted to make his new book better known. In any case, he knowingly let himself be caught in the system. Two weeks later, the Rumilly brought him on a little further:

"We have here a huge and haunting question, namely the question of French exiles hunted down by the purges and who have found refuge in Canada as best they could. Communist sympathizers, the Jewish element and fanatical English are seeking their deportation."[40]

Then Rumilly went on to explain the struggle waged over the last few years by his friends in order to prevent the expulsion of the best-known fugitive, Count de Bernonville. Public opinion in French Canada, he said, was squarely in favour of Bernonville. However, people in Canada were less adept than people in France at seeing nuances between Pétain and de Gaulle. In short, "wavering between de Gaulle and Pétain would be somewhat disconcerting" for French-Canadian public opinion.[41] Rumilly concluded by making things crystal clear: the lectures given by Rémy would be all the more useful if they contributed to the Bernonville cause being defended by Rumilly's friends.

Hamel was more suspicious of Rémy. He would have preferred that his friend Weygand be invited, or again Isorni - but why Rémy? Hamel wanted to be sure that Rémy did not end up coming to Canada to cry "Vive de Gaulle et vive Pétain."[42] He checked Rémy out by contacting journalists friends working for right-wing newspapers in France. He had been badly burned by his own recent troubles, and now expressed his worries to Rumilly:

> "After everything that I said about de Gaulle, I can't see sponsoring a gentleman who would come presenting flowers to de Gaulle and trying to convince us that de Gaulle hadn't acted like a rebel against legitimate authority in his country, that he did not bear partial or even total responsibility for Mers el Kebir and for Dakar, that he had not plunged France in anarchy during the Liberation and that the purges were not a succession of assassinations and robberies." 43

On August 31, Philippe Hamel drove Rémy back against the wall. Hamel was already seriously considering blocking the plan altogether. He was afraid that this lecture tour would strengthen support for de Gaulle and he said as much in his letter to Rémy:

> "If you were to come to Canada to praise Pétain and to ignore de Gaulle, or better yet to denounce the latter, then you would be doing a tremendous service to the truth and you would be welcomed with enthusiasm." 44

The negotiations stopped, however, and the idea was abandoned.

FOOTNOTES

1. Verdict of the Superior Court of Montreal, made by Justice Louis Cousineau, February 21, 1949 (RR; ANQ; 14).

2. In his Côte des Neiges apartment, Bernonville was a neighbour of Jean Vinant, who would later become president of the France-Canada Chamber of Commerce in Paris. He was said to be a notorious Pétainist. His brother Georges, president of the French Chamber of Commerce in Montreal and an importer of Guerlain perfumes and pharmaceutical products, was every bit his equal in this respect. Along with the vice president of this latter Chamber of Commerce, a certain Ducros, they were the most vehement defenders of Bernonville. They went so far as to threaten their opponents with job dismissals. They often worked through a journalist at *La Presse* called Major.

3. *Le Canada*, February 22, 1949.

4. Ibid., February 22, 1949.

5. Letter from Conrad Bérubé to Louis Saint Laurent, September 12, 1948 (LST; NAC).

6. Letter from Jacques Rousseau to Louis Cecile, January 26, 1949.

7. Roland Haumont met Allister Stewart several times during the Bernonville affair. Stewart struck Haumont as a rigorous Presbyterian Scotsman, with a strong and austere mind.

8. *The Herald*, February 23, 1949 and *Maclean's*, November 15, 1951.

9. *Le Devoir*, February 23, 1949.

10. Letter from Robert Rumilly to Pierre Boutang, *Aspects de la France et du monde*, 1949 (RR; ANQ; 17).

11. "Le cas Bernonville", text of debates in the House of Commons on February 24, 1949, reprinted as a brochure by the École sociale populaire (RR; ANQ; 14).

12. *La Patrie*, February 25, 1949.

13. *Le Canada*, March 11, 1949.

14. Ibid.

15. Secret telegramme from Georges Vanier to Louis Saint Laurent, March 12, 1949 (LST; ANC).

16. Letter from Victor Keyserling to Robert Rumilly, March 1, 1949 (RR; ANQ; 12).

17. Letter from André Laurendeau to Robert Rumilly, August 19, 1949 (RR; ANQ; 12).

18. Notes made by Robert Rumilly (RR; ANQ; 14).

19. Letter from Roger Ouimet to Jacques de Bernonville, January 27, 1950 (RR; ANQ; 14).

20. Archives of the Canadian Jewish Congress in Montreal. Probably the February 22, 1950 edition of *L'action catholique*.

21. *Le Canada*, March 3, 1950.

22. Letter from Philippe Hamel to Robert Rumilly, March 4, 1950 (RR; ANQ; 14).

23. Letter from Jean-François Pouliot to Robert Rumilly, March 11, 1950 (RR; ANQ; 14).

24. Letter from Robert Rumilly to Paul-Edmond Gagnon, March 11, 1950 (RR; ANQ; 14).

25. Letter from Anatole Vanier to Émilien Rochette, March 13, 1950 (RR; ANQ; 14).

26. Letter from J.-A. Mongrain to Prime Minister Louis St-Laurent, reproduced in the press, March 30, 1950 (DB; ACJC).

27. *L'action catholique*, April 1, 1950.

28. Letter from Guy Frégault to Robert Rumilly, April 14, 1950 (RR; ANQ; 14).

29. Letter from Adrien Pouliot to Robert Rumilly, April 14, 1950 (RR; ANQ; 14).

30. List of 143 people having signed the petition sent to Mr. Harris, April 17, 1950 (RR; ANQ; 14).

31. *Le Devoir*, May 2, 1950.

32. Letter from Anatole Vanier to Louis Saint Laurent, June 8, 1950 (RR; ANQ; 14).

33. Letter from Anatole Vanier to Senator Thomas Vien, March 6, 1950 (RR; ANQ; 14).

34. Letter from Commander A. Quivaux to Camillien Houde, March 25, 1949 (RR; ANQ; 14).

35. Microfilmed statement made by Abel Bonnard, March 30, 1949 (RR; ANQ; 14).

36. Letter from Jean-Marc Léger to Robert Rumilly, January 24, 1950 (RR; ANQ; 14).

37. Letter from Robert Rumilly to Jean-Marc Léger, February 1, 1950 (RR;ANQ; 10).

38. Letter from Philippe Hamel to Robert Rumilly, August 28, 1950 (RR; ANQ; 14).

39. Letter from Colonel Rémy (France) to Robert Rumilly, August 6, 1950 (RR; ANQ; 10).

40. Letter from Robert Rumilly to Colonel Rémy, August 16, 1950 (RR; ANQ; 14).

41. Ibid.

42. Letter from Philippe Hamel to Robert Rumilly, August 16, 1950 (RR; ANQ; 10).

43. Letter from Philippe Hamel to Robert Rumilly, August 28, 1950 (RR; ANQ; 14).

44. Letter from Philippe Hamel to Colonel Rémy, August 31, 1950 (RR; ANQ; 14).

Chapter VII

A new Riel affair?

The committee had failed in its efforts to invite pro-Pétain spokes-men from France. It now gathered together whatever forces it already had. In January 1951, Jacques de Bernonville's stay in Canada entered its fifth year. And the future was as unsure as ever.

Rumilly was the pillar of the committee and well aware how weak it was. He stepped up his efforts to coax and revive Pétainist sentiment among French Canadians. He admitted however that the way French Canadians were inclined to fall into a slump was due to "an instinctive and deep-seated feeling among the people".[1]

If only he could count on the support of the Quebec government. Premier Maurice Duplessis had been favourable to the movement at first, but had later abandoned it, although he let some of his deputies reactivate it on occasion. Rumilly felt alone. He said one day to Victor Keyserling that federal ministers would eventually notice that he was thrashing about with only a handful of friends.[2] The historian recognized how many divisions he had:

"On the one side is Jewry, Freemasonry, Communism, Christian Democracy, the Socialists, the hate-filled bureaucracy, the Liberal government, Tory fanaticism and the opportunism of well-thinking people.

"And on the other side, I am all alone with a few friends (...) you cannot imagine how much time, worries and even money I have devoted to this cause."[3]

The collaborator's lawyers had performed miracles. For a year now, they had harassed the bureaucrats and multiplied the legal means at their disposal. Things dragged out, from the committee of inquiry to the committee of appeal. The bureaucrats were all the more furious, since they had known Bernonville's true past from the very beginning of the affair, and even before it was splashed all over the newspapers.

The cabinet wanted to justify the expulsion order. So it allowed public pressure to grow, by allowing the bureaucrats to explain that Bernonville was wanted in France for treason. Nothing much happened however. The problems the bureaucracy had been getting caught up in since January 1950 had to end. A firm decision by the prime minister was needed, some bureaucrats thought. Understandably, St. Laurent had sought to keep his distance. In January 1951, the ball came back into his court and he was asked to act. He no longer had any choice and finally moved.

On February 8, 1951, the government shook itself awake and decided to come out openly in support of its bureaucrats. The deportation order in effect against Bernonville had to be respected. Canadian law did not allow any person to enter Canada who had been convicted of high treason or of conspiring against His Majesty. Ottawa declared that any person having in time of war helped the enemies of His Majesty was subject to this law.

The count had 60 days to leave. If he didn't comply with the order, he would be forced to leave unless ... unless, of course, he did not contest this decision again in the courts.

Once again, the familiar old scenario was repeated. Bernonville's lawyers issued a writ of *habeus corpus* in order to bring his case before the courts. The defence committee meanwhile got moving, although without as much enthusiasim as before.

Indeed, there were fewer supporters now around Jacques de Bernonville. Some people were tired out by this never-ending affair; others had more and more serious doubts about the crimes attributed to Bernonville; still others, like Philippe Hamel, didn't have the physical stamina to fight anymore.

In Ottawa, the Conservative deputy Henri Courtemanche came to the defence of Bernonville. On February 8, he rose in the federal Parliament and slammed the French Communists. He said they had fabricated all the accusations made against Bernonville. Quebec, he said, wanted to welcome this Frenchman.

" We never hear about immigrants who have been allowed to stay in Canada although they enter this country with false passports. Why make it a crime for de Bernonville to have sought refuge in Quebec, when not a single voice was raised in this province asking for his deportation. Could it be that Quebec does not have the right to choose the sort of immigrants it wants?" [4]

Meanwhile, the Liberal member for Bonaventure, Bona Arsenault, put out feelers in Ottawa. He was thinking of proposing a special bill clearing the government of current legislation and permitting the permanent and legal residence in Canada of Count de Bernonville.

René Chaloult, still a deputy in Quebec's Legislative Assembly, felt isolated, since some of his parliamentary colleagues were willing to support him behind the scenes but refused to speak openly in favour of the Frenchman.

In mid-February 1951, René Chaloult gave a speech in the Quebec assembly that left no doubt about his convictions. He charged that Ottawa was flying in the face of public opinion in Quebec, by refusing to grant Bernonville asylum, unlike the United States and other countries, which had granted asylum to the Patriotes of 1837-38. Meanwhile, the bureaucracy was organizing a massive wave of immigration in order to drown and assimilate the French-Canadian population.

More than five years after Pétain's internment on Ile d'Yeu had begun, Chaloult showed he was just as fervent a supporter as ever:

" We refuse to believe in the justice of a régime that keeps in its prisons a large part of the French élite, a régime that continues to hound an old man of 93 years, the hero of Verdun, the illustrious Marshal Pétain, whose interminable agony disturbs the entire universe." [5]

Among Rumilly's allies were many students at the Université de Montréal. On March 13, 1951, Denis Lazure, president of the AGEUM, the students' association, sent a telegramme in support of Bernonville to Prime Minister Louis St. Laurent. The motion had been presented by a delegate from the Faculty of Philosophy, André Payette. The AGEUM spoke on behalf of 3,000 students, and asked that " Jacques de Bernonville be granted permission to remain in Canada with his family, the way political refugees are admitted to all countries." [6]

A week later, Pierre Asselin, St. Laurent's private secretary, let the students know that the charges facing Bernonville were extremely serious. So far, incomplete information about this Frenchman had been published. The prime minister however knew the whole story and could not reverse the decision of his bureaucrats and ministers.

The students did not give up easily. André Payette wrote that the opposition to Bernonville was a plot by "Canadian Communists, who want to hand over to their brothers, the French Communists, a man of value who is both Catholic and magnanimous."[7] Payette then told Rumilly the name of a student who had seemed hostile during a lecture Rumilly had given at the university.

The organizational breakdown that Rumilly feared could also be seen among the nationalist associations. Only a few groups, such as the Ligue des Patriotes, took position. Bernonville was a persecuted hero.

Then suddenly, support came from an unexpected quarter: Claude-Henri Grignon, who was not only an irrepressible pamphleteer but also a novelist and author of the bestseller *Un homme et son péché*. The book told the story of a miser's misappropriation of funds in rural Quebec. *Séraphin*, a feature film based on the novel, had just been released. And since 1939, radio listeners had been tuning in to a radio version of *Un homme et son péché*.

Grignon had often been at daggers drawn with Rumilly, but this time was literally on the same wavelength, since the radio station CKAC broadcast their respective talks on Bernonville close together.

Grignon was deeply indignant when he came before the microphone. Up till now, he said, he had abstained from getting involved in the affair, since there would be a happy ending sooner or later. But things had gone too far. The ministers were behaving like their bureaucrats, and wanted to drag Bernonville, a faithful servant of the Marshal, before the enemies of Charles Maurras. "The Resistance did nothing to save France," he said, "It was Pétain along with his servants."[8] Grignon also dealt with the theme of immigration:

"Isn't it true that we receive bad stew within our walls, and shysters, and imported wogs from the four corners of the world? Why then shouldn't we accept a political refugee, an honourable Frenchman who is worthy of our ancestors and of our best-loved traditions."

Rumilly followed suit a few days later. His talk was financed by the Union Nationale and was part of a series held on the subject of provincial autonomy. On this occasion, Rumilly claimed to be as an impartial historian, and drew parallels between the history of Quebec and the Bernonville affair. The two talks, given in February and March 1951, were like an anthology of the arguments advanced over the previous two and a half years. He associated the Bernonville affair with the Patriotes of 1837-38. He then referred to the Louis Riel affair, when the francophone Métis leader of the Canadian West was hanged after leading the Métis insurrection, which had created a rift between English Canadians and French Canadians at the end of the 19th century.

Rumilly also spoke of the victims of the French Revolution and of the way the English had manipulated Joan of Arc's trial. He also explained how religious communities had saved Bernonville from the purges (although they might have preferred not to be reminded of the fact). He even hinted that French-Canadian religious might have helped save the count.

Rumilly then evoked Jacques de Bernonville's mysticism. He spoke deceitfully of the role of the Maintenance of Order in occupied France, which he claimed had been set up by Marshal Pétain in order to protect the population against acts of terrorism.

Finally, Rumilly pilloried Louis St. Laurent. He accused the prime minister of obeying the orders of Communists and of helping increase the prison population in France. Rumilly had written a biography of Wilfrid Laurier, the former Liberal prime minister of Canada. But he now called for a boycott of the Liberals in the next elections.[9]

A few days later, Rumilly received a note scribbled by one of St. Laurent's supporters. The letter delivered a blunt message, in the down-to-earth language of the people. The note shows that the Liberals wanted to avoid any electoral damage, and also betrays the xenophobic sentiments of the time regarding people from French.

"Filthy traitor, if you think that everybody in Quebec is in favour of the French traitor Bernonville, you have another thing coming. The filthy wretched dogs who kill their brothers, the damn Canadians like the old bastard Pétain, hang those buggers high. You are too much of a coward to go live in your beggar of a country. It's like men who come bawling for food, then spit on us after. In your country, they do nothing but beg, they haven't got enough brains to form a government that will last 40 years like us Liberals. Talk about that on the radio, you Chaloult Hamel Arcand Hitler 'your' gang. Long live St. Laurent and the Liberals. Hang Bernonville high."[10]

A more prosaic answer was given by Senator T.D. Bouchard. When he heard "this foreigner with his dry words and halting speech braying on the radio" his heart skipped a beat. According to Bouchard, Rumilly was part of a clique of separatists and reactionaries trying to cause dissension among Canadians. The senator, an unconditional federalist, was also indignant about the treatment reserved for St. Laurent.

"It is as clear as day that this lecturer hasn't been hired to popularize history; he gets his paycheck for disfiguring history in order to harm the supporters of Canadian unity and promote the cause of those who want to separate our province from Confederation and the British Commonwealth to make us straight Québécois. This policy of national suicide means we would be much more at the mercy of these reactionaries than we already are." [11]

THE MAN IS A NUISANCE

Rumilly did what he could on the radio, but support for Bernonville quietly returned to what it had been at the outset, small and active pro-Vichy groups. Some nationalists admitted in private that they were no longer interested in the affair although they claimed to still sympathize with Bernonville. The press no longer made a big thing about it, the way it had in Fall 1948.

Dr. Damien St. Pierre, an active pro-Bernonville supporter, sought to reassure Rumilly. "Obviously, I am in favour or pro-Bernonville in spite of everything." [12] Rumilly tried to convince himself that Bernonville's deportation simply couldn't take place. Surely the trench-warfare he had been waging these last few years would end in victory. According to Rumilly, trying Commander de Bernonville in France would have dreadful ramifications and would mean relaunching the civil war.

St. Laurent, however, was not impressed by threats of an electoral boycott. He had easily won the previous elections and saw that the affair was fizzling out. It was a whole new St. Laurent appearing before Bernonville. On March 19, 1951, St. Laurent's private secretary sent a blunt refusal in his name to Bernonville's successive pleas. However, St. Laurent suggested an honourable way out for the Frenchman. His secretary said that a return to France was not the only choice. It might be possible for Bernonville to choose other destinations. Perhaps other countries might be willing to take him in. [13]

But the worst was yet to come for Bernonville's protectors. On March 27, 1951, René Chaloult informed Rumilly of a new blow. Defending Bernonville was becoming much more difficult. The deputy was deeply disturbed, and wrote:

"I contacted Noël Dorion, one of de B.'s most loyal friends. He said he was extremely worried about everything he had heard about the file. Dorion says that Bernonville not only received money from the Germans, but was also a member of the SS shock troops."[14]

Chaloult continued:

"Dr. Hamel told me this morning for the first time that Commander Quivault, who is loyal to the Marshal, told him to beware of de B. because he had accepted money from the Germans while loyally fulfilling his orders. For the commander that was no reason to blame de B., but simply something for Dr. Hamel to be careful about."

This piece of news was extremely embarrassing. After all, in French Canada, Hitler's Germany was the enemy that many French Canadians had fought against. One senses in Chaloult's letter that he wanted to keep his new knowledge secret. "I imagine you are aware of all these facts," Chaloult wrote sarcastically to Rumilly. "For my part, they don't impress me and I am ready to spread my name around everywhere and go all-out to defend this affair."

The deputy admitted however that his supporters were not of the same mind. Some of the most active ones were reluctant to continue. Some, like Noël Dorion, didn't want to see their names in printed tracts of the committee. Others, like Émilien Rochette, accepted to continue, although they knew about the accusation. This latter group was in the minority however.

As for Dr. Hamel, he planned to continue, but his state of health sapped his energy. On March 28, 1951, Hamel sent a letter to Bernonville, sharing some distressing information about him. Bernonville had to help him by telling him the whole truth. Hamel was already beginning to think of how to turn the situation around:

"For God's sake, give us the means to refute the accusations that you were part of the German Milice and received German pay (...).

"Nobody will ever succeed in convincing me that you did anything other than heroically serve your country, but I insist that your friends be in a position to defend you by explaining what may *prima facie* seem to be treason."[15]

In Spring 1951, the Committee for the Defence of French Refugees had shrunk in size. Among its members were the federal MPs Bona Arsenault, Henri Courtemanche and Paul-Edmond Gagnon and the provincial deputies René Chaloult and Alfred Plourde. The latter, a Union Nationale deputy since 1948, was the one had who first taken in Bernonville and given him a job in his lumber company in St. Pacôme in 1947.

Among the other members were Antoine Masson, who claimed to have been saved in France thanks to the good offices of Commander de Bernonville, André Payette, a student at the Université de Montréal, Mayor Mongrain of Trois Rivières, Damien St. Pierre of Ottawa, Anatole Vanier of Montreal, and Rumilly himself.[16]

When Léo Guindon of the Alliance des Professeurs Catholiques de Montréal was invited to join the committee, he bowed out due to a lack of time. The year before, he had signed a petition supporting the count, along with other prominent figures. "I believe," he wrote on March 30, 1951 to Rumilly, "that I have enough problems of my own without taking on the problems of others."[17] The curate of Bernonville's parish would not sit on the committee, but provided a financial contribution to help cover the count's legal costs. The priest said that Bernonville was one of his most fervent parishioners.

Bernonville was now in the insurance business and got a certain amount of support from his workmates. On May 6, 1951 in Montreal, during the annual convention of the Union des Compagnies d'Assurances, Bernonville was invited to relate his war experiences. He took the opportunity to blast some members of the French colony, thinking no doubt of Free French veterans. But what really attracted attention was his statement that Pétain and Franco were the two greatest diplomats of the last war.

During the same convention, Yves Benoit, a psychologist and the author of the book *Comment vaincre sa timidité* (*How to fight shyness*), heaped praise on Bernonville during his presentation. He cast him as the victim of "Jewish Freemasonry" which was hunting him down even in Montreal.[18] As the leaders of the Canadian Jewish Congress observed in their memos, it is interesting to note that neither *Le Devoir* nor *Montréal-Matin* republished this phrase.[19] *Le Canada* featured it however.

In France, Bernonville still enjoyed the support of his mysterious friend Reynaud from Lyon. According to Reynaud, with the French

President Vincent Auriol soon to visit Canada, it would be a good time for the count's followers to vent their indignation at the Marshal's imprisonment.

The president's arrival in Canada in Spring 1951 did not provoke the sort of reactions Reynaud had been hoping for. However, Maurice Ferro, a journalist for *Le Monde* based in Washington, covered the visit of the president and did a write-up on French Canada in 1951.

On his arrival from Washington, the diplomatic correspondent noticed right away that conversations in Quebec started in English. Customs officials in their navy-blue uniforms greeted him in English. As he traveled about Quebec, however, a church belfry and especially the colourful French accents reminded him of the province's French roots. He said he had decoded this way of speaking, by recalling the dialects of Normandy and Picardy from the time of Louis XIV. He also noted that religion was the guardian of customs and of language.

During his trip, Ferro met a "very highly-placed Montreal official". The journalist couldn't give the name of the person, but it could well have been the mayor of Montreal, Camillien Houde. The latter spoke to him about the war and particularly about his own point of view on the issues of the time. One wonders whether Rumilly or Houde was the more likely to have spoken these words:

"In Quebec, we are on the far Right. We do not want to make war against a régime which has the same views as us, even as bad a régime as Hitler's. England dragged us into two wars - against our will. These were adventures in which we had everything to lose and nothing to gain. They cost us dearly." [20]

The journalist was startled by this declaration, and switched to the Bernonville affair. He asked whether the person he was speaking to knew of Bernonville's role in the repression of the Resistance:

"Hadn't the person I was speaking to heard of the plâteau de Glières, of the wretched operation led by the SS under Bernonville's command, in which 400 patriots were killed? He starts to come round, or rather to lay blame on the fact that a retreat started a few days beforehand. Bernonville, he agrees, the man has become an nuisance. Oh! if only he would go to Argentina - leave for another country."

Once the article was published, Bernonville fine-tuned his reply to the newspaper. He astutely used some mistakes concerning his past to discredit the whole article. The newspaper published his letter two months later. [21] Bernonville's plea had four main points: 1. He had never fought in the German ranks (indeed, the militia was not the same thing as the Wehrmacht); 2. He had never run the Milice in Lyon (on a strictly operational level, this was true - his title in Lyon was military governor, which was an administrative façade to cover the Milice); 3. He had never worn a German uniform (this was probably true, since the uniform of the Milice was closer to the uniform of the Chasseurs alpins); 4. He had never commanded operations led by the SS, whether in Glières or anywhere else (in Glières, the supreme command of operations in the field was assigned to Vaugelas; Bernonville could also claim with reason that he did not go to the front with the Germans during the assault of March 26, 1944, since on that particular day at least, he stayed down below to ensure that nobody escaped the trap).

Bernonville's defence consisted of wordplay. But it nonetheless impressed the editors of Le Monde. The newspaper gave him the benefit of the doubt and admitted at the end of his letter that the journalist had not checked all his information first-hand.

A KIDNAP PLOT

During the French president's visit to Canada, Prime Minister St. Laurent was subject to increasingly intense pressure from Canadian veterans. They were outraged at Bernonville's procedural wrangling. They decided to take matters into their own hands.

The following account is worthy of a spy thriller by John Le Carré.[22] Canadian veterans, mainly former airmen who had fought in the European theatre in World War Two, got in touch with one of their former American colleagues, who had since become a prosperous businessman in Texas. The American knew the Milice well. During the war, his airplane had been shot down over France and he had to open his parachute. Members of the Resistance picked him up and saved him from the Milice.

The businessman learned of the interminable drama in Canada, and dreamed up a completely hare-brained plot. Well, not quite so hare-brained, because the Israeli secret service would later use the same idea to lay hands on the Nazi war criminal Adolf Eichmann, then living in Argentina.

The Texan thought of kidnapping Bernonville from his Montreal home and taking him by air to Plattsburgh, on the shores of Lake Champlain in upstate New York. From there, Bernonville would be handed over to French authorities who would take him on a small aircraft to the French islands of St. Pierre and Miquelon in the Gulf of St. Lawrence.

The French veterans Michel Pichard and Roland Haumont were informed of the plan and asked to find an alibi so they could show they were not involved.[23] The plan was too wild to work, however, and was abandoned.

But the American did not give up easily. He declared that he was ready to pay $75,000 up-front in a campaign against St. Laurent if the prime minister didn't quickly send Bernonville back to France.

The threat reached St. Laurent's ears. It was just one more in a long series of rumours, but the prime minister understood the urgency of the situation. He turned to the religious hierarchy of Quebec. A note prepared by one of his advisors examined the role that the clergy of the diocese of Quebec City had played since the French collaborators had arrived in Canada. The note said that the religious had been fooled by the Pétainists into seeing or wanting to see in the Miliciens nothing but good Catholics. The memo continued in a mocking tone, underlining the fact that leading lights in the diocese had hotly taken up the defence of "great Catholics fleeing Communism",[24] who had found a logical landing-place in Quebec, one-time capital of New France.

Many Catholic religious in Quebec, perhaps the majority, had indeed supported the cause of Count de Bernonville's supporters. Among these religious was the historian Canon Lionel Groulx.[25]

There were some exceptions, however, such as the Sulpicians of Montreal, who kept their distance from the affair. The archbishop of Montreal, Mgr. Joseph Charbonneau, maintained silence throughout the affair. Up till his sudden departure from Montreal in 1950, he discreetly let the Free French veterans know he supported their attempts to deport Bernonville. The superior of the Mother House of Sacré Coeur in Longueuil, in Montreal's South Shore suburbs, was more explicit in his opposition to Bernonville. This Dachau survivor declared in one of his sermons: "God said: go, your sins are forgiven. Well, in Bernonville's case, I won't forgive him."[26]

The prime minister was well aware of the influence of ecclesiastical authorities and particularly of the archdiocese of Quebec. Mgr. Maurice Roy was very discreet and had not directly take part in the affair. He may have kept contact with the defence committee via Mgr. Vandry. A letter from Mme. L. Racine to Rumilly suggested as much.

"Mgr. V. (which could also have been Mgr. Valois) recommends discretion over the telephone since he claims we may be under surveillance". [27]

St. Laurent saw Mgr. Roy as the person who could get people to drop the pro-Bernonville campaign. Just before the summer, St. Laurent got in touch with the archbishop, and got right to the point: "Your friends brought him into the country, your friends are going to take him out again". [28] The message, transmitted by T.D. Bouchard, could not have been more clear. The prime minister's message bore fruit and the campaign to defend Bernonville lost some more steam.

Bernonville now felt abandoned on all sides. He therefore followed St. Laurent's advice and sought asylum elsewhere. Even members of his own family no longer believed he had a chance of staying in Canada. They were utterly demoralized, and had recently begun returning to France.

Meanwhile, Bernonville's lawyer, Jacques Perrault, laid the groundwork for a new trial. Bernonville had obtained a second writ of *habeus corpus* and would soon be in court once again. Perrault would plead the defence, while Guy Favreau was getting ready to plead on behalf of the federal government.

In the middle of August, a leak sent journalists racing to Dorval airport, where they witnessed the sudden departure of Jacques de Bernonville. His flight to Brazil had been kept secret, and the take-off was due a few minutes later.

The flight plan of the four-engined aircraft did not call for any stops in the United States. And with reason. The Americans had denied Bernonville permission to land on their soil, even to change planes. (*Le Devoir* interpreted this gesture as a lack of generosity. In fact, the plane developed engine trouble and had to make a short stop.)

At Dorval airport, Bernonville's wife accompanied him to the boarding platform, along with the Brazilian consul in Montreal, his lawyer Jacques Perrault and a few friends.

Perrault defended him to the very last, saying that businessmen in Rio de Janeiro had offered him an interesting job. The count had accepted the offer and was now on his way. According to Perrault, Bernonville did not want to be the cause of dissension among Canadians. In any case, Perrault concluded, Brazil, unlike Canada, was not afraid of France.[29]

The former Milice chief's five-year stay in Canada now ended in complete indifference. There was no anger, there were no protests by any of the organizations involved, although the departure made headlines in practically every newspaper. Without a doubt, Mgr. Roy's orders had something to do with the silence over the affair. In the English-language press, *The Standard* cried good riddance. In an editorial, it recalled the various documents it had published incriminating Bernonville throughout the affair.

A few days before leaving Canada, Bernonville wrote a letter of farewell to his supporters on the defence committee: "I will always keep a marvelous vision of your lovely province of Quebec in full bloom, and of its population which has miraculously kept alive the greatest of our French and Catholic traditions."[30]

The Bernonville affair ended at the very moment that Philippe Pétain died on Ile d'Yeu at the age of 95 years. His death, on July 23, marked both the end of the Bernonville story and its epilogue in Canada. As soon as the marshal died, a group of Vichy supporters, inspired by Rumilly, thought of holding a commemorative mass in his honour. Although some accounts spoke of a large number of people at the mass held in Notre Dame Basilica in Montreal, few people really attended.

The dignitaries present were the hard core of Pétainist sympathizers in Quebec. They included Canadians of French origin, such as Jean Bonnel, Jacques Fichet, Dr. Boussat, Louis Even, Robert Rumilly and some veterans. These Frenchmen thought of themselves first and foremost as Pétainists. They were nationalists to varying degrees.

On the French-Canadian side, some nationalist groups were represented, such as the Société St. Jean Baptiste of Montreal and the Ligue Nationale. Representatives of religious groups such as the Ligue du Sacré-Coeur and the Jesuits were also present. For these groups, Pétainism blended with and enriched their deep nationalist and religious convictions. As soon as he arrived in Montreal in Summer 1951, André Malavoy saw just how important Quebec support for Pétain still was.[31]

These supporters had hit it off with Bernonville over the previous three years. The organizers of the mass had tried to bring in new faces, but to no avail.

On November 15, five days after the funeral service, the Toronto magazine *Maclean's* published a devastating indictment of Bernonville, signed by the journalist McKenzie Porter. The feature article laid out all the facts. It established down to the smallest details what

Bernonville had been up to between 1940 and 1944, during the German occupation of France. Porter did not merely recount Bernonville's collaborationist past. A fair number of documents had already been published by English-language newspapers during the affair. Actually, Porter's contribution was to meticulously expose the scandal of Bernonville's life.

Relying on documents provided by veterans of the Resistance, Porter proved beyond a shadow of a doubt what Bernonville's crimes were during the period. Mayor Camillien Houde had tried to convince him not to publish the facts, by accusing him of wanting to send Bernonville to certain death. The journalist did not give up however. Strangely enough, he admitted having collected the damning evidence two years beforehand. He justified not publishing it right away because of the legal proceedings that got underway in 1950.

THE ASSASSINATION OF JACQUES DE BERNONVILLE

As soon as Bernonville arrived in Brazil, he gave a press conference where he admitted having served in the Milice, but claimed that he had left it afterwards. While waiting to find a better place to stay, he stayed at St. Anthony's Monastery in Rio de Janeiro. The former imperial family of Brazil, the Braganzas, were supposed to receive him, but quickly distanced themselves from this compromising individual.

The Canadian authorities kept a close watch on him, via their ambassador in Brazil. The secretary of state for External Affairs of Canada called for discreet inquiries to be made into his whereabouts. The diplomat regularly sent word to Ottawa of the comings and goings of the Frenchman. The bureaucrats wanted to know in particular whether he had any plans of returning to Canada. They wanted to block his reappearance at any cost, since it could open up a rift between the "two solitudes". There was some indication that a return to Canada was in the works. The lawyer Jacques Perrault maintained contacts with Bernonville and waited for fresh instructions.

The fugitive also remained in contact with Mme. Racine. Also keeping up correspondence with him were other people, such as René Chaloult, Anatole Vanier, the federal MP Jean-François Pouliot and Robert Rumilly. Indeed, Rumilly, who was always generous towards his comrades in arms, even wired money to Brazil, which was greatly appreciated by Bernonville.

However, the chances of returning diminished. Canada seemed to be getting tougher and no longer quite so welcoming for collaborators. Other fugitives established contact with Rumilly in the hopes of reaching America. Rumilly had to temper their enthusiasm and explain to them how difficult it was to settle here. Canada, he told them, was not the El Dorado they longed for.

Even so, a man who had worked under Philippe Henriot, Vichy's secretary of Information, appealed to Rumilly. Georges Grossis wrote from Mansourah, Egypt, inquiring about the possibility of working at Laval University. He was teaching French in a high school and wondered whether it was true that the Quebec university recruited people from France each year.

He had been condemned to death and was worried that the Anglo-French crisis over the Suez Canal might have repercussions on his stay in Egypt. He felt he was not only floundering in an ocean of foreigners but also misunderstood by fellow French citizens residing in Egypt.[32]

The partial amnesty decreed by France in 1951 offered the possibility of a return to Canada for former collaborators, but only if they entered legally and with a valid passport. That was the case of Gaston Bonjour, an engineer in Avignonet. The amnesty law repealing the penalty of national disgrace for people sentenced to less than 15 years meant that he could get his papers back. As a result, he planned to leave France quite lawfully. Bonjour explained his decision to Rumilly by saying that he couldn't stand living in France. He was up against Judeo-Gaullist terror and the veterans of the FFI, the Forces Française Intérieures which he called the Fripouilles Françaises et Internationales (French and International Scoundels). Now that France was back in the hands of Jewry, Bonjour wanted to just wanted to leave.

"(...) this country is no longer ours. We don't amount to anything anymore. The Jews have taken over. And they have perverted everything, trampled on everything, corrupted everything, defiled everything. Your family, your personal friends, your daily surroundings, everything is completely impregnated with the messianic, sickly, devilish, moneygrubbing and tearful, fickle and indifferent, naive and childish mentality of the Jew (...) Everything is contaminated. Everything is decaying. Very few healthy minds manage to escape." [33]

On May 26, 1952, in his last letter to Rumilly, Gaston Bonjour said he was just about to leave for his new life in Canada. To help him prepare his departure, Rumilly had provided a wealth of practical advice.

In Brazil, meanwhile, there were some surprising developments. In March 1952, the French government, via its ambassador, formally requested the extradition of Bernonville so that he could be tried in his country. A new Bernonville affair got underway in Brazil.[34] This meant court cases once again and the snail's pace of justice as the buck was passed from one official to another.

The Brazilian press called Bernonville a "gauleiter" and a "Nazi executioner". Bernonville defended himself by saying that it was necessary to obey the Marshal. In the meantime, an unfavourable court decision came down, opening the way to deportation. Bernonville was alarmed, and contacted his Canadian friends to get them to send documents casting him in a positive light. Bernonville asked Anatole Vanier to send him among other things a copy of an English-language Communist newspaper that demanded that he be deported.

In 1955, Bernonville was deeply concerned that he might lose his new trial. Goaded by the French diplomatic corps, Brazilian newspapers waged a far more vigorous war against Bernonville than had been the case with Canadian newspapers four years before. Bernonville had his back to the wall and wrote to Rumilly:

"Here, there are no limits to the insults: one of the cruelest 'gauleiters' in the history of Nazi-Fascism, thief, murderer of hundreds of 'patriots', arsonist, plunderer, torturer, a man without a single French or Christian feeling in his heart... so cruel that the occupying forces themselves asked that he be 'replaced', accepted millions to betray his country. That is some of the 'official' information released by France's ambassador." [35]

On October 1956, after many new legal developments, the federal Supreme Court rejected France's extradition request. From now on, wrote Tiago, alias Jacques Benoit, that is Jacques de Bernonville, nobody could touch him. Brazil offered a safe haven. In 1968, he reminded Robert Rumilly of the words of a religious protecting his friend Paul Touvier, "All in all, Providence has guided your steps well." [36]

Bernonville maintained contacts with Rumilly, although the contacts diminished with time. The reason for the exchange of correspondence in 1968 was that the French historian Robert Aron was researching the French purges in order to write a multi-volume history about them. He therefore got in touch with Rumilly, to retrace the story of Jacques de Bernonville and everything he had experienced in Canada.

Rumilly looked on Aron's request with extreme suspicion. He started going through Aron's work, on the lookout for the slightest pejorative adjective about the victims of the French purges.

He expressed his reservations to Aron and showed his colours:

"I have met several victims of the purges and I defended them here. They were all admirable people, who had been sustained by a burst of generosity. We should pay tribute to the courageous volunteers who went to fight in Russia - in Russia! when the game seemed to be over."[37]

An old acquaintance, Jacques Isorni, thought Rumilly was duty-bound to meet Aron. Even if the "undertakings" of the French historian did not entirely please him, the lawyer said that it was an opportunity that should not be missed. "It could even be an opportunity to help him to avoid making new errors."[38] Aron ultimately did meet Rumilly in Montreal, and the two cooperated on themes linked to the role of French Canadians in World War Two.

On May 5, 1972, while chatting at his Town of Mt. Royal residence with the young historian Pierre Trépanier,[39]Robert Rumilly received a phone call that ended an epoch. His friend Jacques de Bernonville had just been assassinated in Brazil.

A few days beforehand, on April 27, Wilson Francisco de Oliveira killed Bernonville, in his apartment. The young man was the son of Bernonville's cleaning-lady and, as he told the police, under the influence of alcohol and hashish. The body was discovered, tied up, lying before a portrait of Pétain. The man was nearly 75 years old. The political significance of the assassination was hard to establish, although Bernonville had come into contact with former Nazis hiding in Brazil and neighbouring countries.[40]

Just before his death, Bernonville had indicated that he wanted to write his side of the story of the Occupation. His death coincided with the discovery in nearby Bolivia of Klaus Altmann, alias Klaus Barbie, who had fled to Latin America in 1951, the same year as Bernonville left Canada.

The news was front-page news in Brazil. The newspaper *O Globo* ran a huge headline on its front page. The news was merely alluded to in French and Canadian newspapers.

FOOTNOTES

1. Letter from Robert Rumilly to Guy Boussac, December 21, 1949 (RR; ANQ; 8).
2. Letter from Robert Rumilly to Victor Keyserling, March 9, 1949 (RR; ANQ; 12).
3. Ibid.
4. Debates of the House of Commons, *Hansard*, Thursday, February 8, 1951 (RR; ANQ; 14).
5. *Le Devoir*, February 14, 1951.
6. Notes by Denis Lazure, president of the AGEUM, March 13, 1951 (RR; ANQ; 14).
7. Statement signed by André Payette (RR; ANQ; 14).
8. Transcript of a radio talk given by Claude-Henri Grignon, February 25, 1951 (RR; ANQ; 14).
9. Transcript of two CKAC radio talks given by Robert Rumilly in February and March 1951 (RR; ANQ; 14).
10. Manuscript copy of an unsigned letter sent to Robert Rumilly (RR; ANQ; 14).
11. *Le Haut-Parleur*, February 24, 1951.
12. Letter from Damien Saint-Pierre to Robert Rumilly, February 23, 1951 (RR; ANQ; 12).
13. *The Globe and Mail*, January 14, 1984.
14. Letter from René Chaloult to Robert Rumilly, March 27, 1951 (RR; ANQ; 14).
15. Letter from Philippe Hamel to Jacques de Bernonville, March 28, 1951 (RR; ANQ; 14).
16. Communiqué issued by the Committee for the Defence of French Political Refugees, probably Spring 1951 (RR; ANQ; 14).
17. Letter from Léo Guindon to Robert Rumilly, March 30, 1951 (RR; ANQ; 14).
18. *Le Canada*, May 7, 1951.
19. Press review sent by D. Kirshnblatt to Saul Hayes, May 15, 1951 (DB; ACJC).
20. *Le Monde*, May 16, 1951.
21. Ibid., July 18, 1951.
22. Interview with Roland Haumont, Spring 1994, Montreal.
23. According to Roland Haumont, the head of the Royal Canadian Mounted Police at the time told Colonel Pichard, Étienne Kraft and Haumont himself that they should drop by his place if the kidnapping took place, so that they had a solid alibi. The RCMP chief had heard that Hilaire Beauregard, the provincial police chief, had plans to arrest them on the spot.
24. Confidential notes addressed to Louis Saint Laurent (LST; NAC).

25. Letter from Robert Rumilly to Canon Lionel Groulx, April 20, 1950; Lionel Groulx Collection, P1/A, Centre de recherches Lionel Groulx, Montreal.

26. Interview with Roland Haumont, Spring 1984, Montreal.

27. Letter from L. Racine to Robert Rumilly, April 26, 1950 (RR; ANQ; 10).

28. Interview with Roland Haumont, Spring 1984, Montreal.

29. *Le Devoir*, August 18, 1951.

30. Letter from Jacques de Bernonville to the members of the Committee for the Defence of French Political Refugees, August 15, 1951 (RR; ANQ; 12).

31. Interview with André Malavoy, Spring 1994, Montreal.

32. Letters from Georges Grossis (Mansourah, Egypt) to Robert Rumilly, January 3, 1951 (RR; ANQ; 13) and June 6, 1951 (RR; ANQ; 8).

33. Letter from Gaston Bonjour (Avignoret, France) to Robert Rumilly, May 26, 1952 (RR; ANQ; 13).

34. In Brazil, the attack against Bernonville was mainly organized by Maurice Duclos (alias St. Jacques). He was a former member of the Cagoule who had joined de Gaulle in 1940. He served brilliantly in the Underground, and received the Croix de la Libération, the Médaille de la Résistance and the Military Cross. He had known Bernonville well in the Cagoule. After the war, Duclos moved to Brazil. (Interview with Roland Haumont.) On Duclos, see Henri Noguères, *Histoire de la Résistance en France*, Paris, Laffont, 1972.

35. Letter from Jacques de Bernonville (Rio de Janeiro, Brazil) to Robert Rumilly, February 7, 1955 (RR; ANQ; 13).

36. Letter from Jacques de Bernonville (Rio de Janeiro, Brazil) to Robert Rumilly, March 8, 1968 (RR; ANQ; 14).

37. Letter from Robert Rumilly to Robert Aron, January 22, 1968 (RR; ANQ; 12).

38. Letter from Jacques Isorni to Robert Rumilly, February 5, 1968 (RR; ANQ; 12).

39. Pierre Trépanier, *Robert Rumilly, historien engagé*, 30 p. (RR; ANQ; 8).

40. This theory was explored by William Stevenson in his book *The Bormann Brotherhood*.

CONCLUSION

QUEBEC-FAMILY-FATHERLAND

I s it possible to come to some understanding of this story, on the basis of a short work of micro-history? Taken by itself, the events seem to have been fairly banal. A Nazi collaborator settled in Quebec and a media campaign sprang up to prevent his deportation. This kind of situation is a common occurrence in our own day. But it is important to place the story in context; after all, the press blew the Bernonville affair out of proportion in the hopes of selling more newspapers and raking in greater profits.

The Bernonville affair may be used, however, to probe Quebec society at a given moment of its history, on the eve moreover of a huge transformation — the Quiet Revolution. Indeed, the Bernonville affair gave latent opinions a concrete public form. It was far more revealing that appeared at first sight.

Bernonville arrived in 1946 in a community which had not understood much about the European war and its political aims. This man's record was more or less grasped by the first people to defend him, during his clandestine period. Debating the ins-and-outs of Vichy and the Collaboration struck many people as a futile kind of moral argument. For them all, however, Bernonville was a Pétainist who had steadfastly remained loyal to the Marshal.

The Canadian friends at his side before the affair broke out in September 1948 formed a small intransigent group consisting of two branches. The first branch consisted of moderately nationalistic Frenchmen, who had an unconditional admiration for the Marshal. They kept the flame burning for ideological reasons, but also for practical ones. One had been Pétain's chef at Verdun. The second branch consisted of nationalists with reactionary political ideas, such as Philippe Hamel. They were all doubtless aware of the acts Bernonville had committed against some of his fellow countrymen, but there was not much fuss about the acts, since they had targeted Communists. This second branch did not in reality consider such acts to be crimes.

As for Bernonville's involvement with the Nazis, some may have suspected he had been so involved; but they took a view contrary to that held by their opponents during the war in France. From compromise to compromise, they complacently slipped, until they ended up justifying, in the name of a fundamentalist Catholicism and anti-Communism, acts which they would have condemned three years before. Here, on the shores of the St. Lawrence, there was a delayed-action movement, that justified State collaboration and masked collaborationism. Everything was done in the name of the Marshal. Collaboration, at least as it was perpetrated by the Milice, found favour here thanks to blind support for Pétain.

The support given to the count by his first defenders was not a product of solidarity with Nazis or with National-Socialism. Bernonville himself was a nationalist of the school of Maurras who had fought the Germans during World War One, and as a Royalist doubtless kept his distance from the Nazis. Still. that did not prevent this extreme-right-wing warrior from closely collaborating with the Gestapo to eliminate their common enemies, the Communists.

During the war, while certain French autonomist movements were attracted to Nazism, there was no such drift in Quebec. This drift toward Nazism was the consequence of a combination of circumstances which did not in any case prevail in Quebec. Hitler sought to seduce movements established in France, a territory occupied by Germany. He managed to attract some individuals associated with the autonomist cause. The most likely ones to respond to this attention were in the Corsican, Breton and Alsatian autonomist movements. Some of these people even associated the success of their claims with a Nazi victory. For Hitler, the operation had more to do with strategy than with any ideological affinity. A Nazi triumph in Europe would probably have seen these fair-weather friends disappear. The historian Francis Arzalier has carefully studied this whole question and he concludes that autonomism does not naturally lead to Fascism.[1]

In Quebec, the nationalists of the Bloc Populaire were briefly courted from a distance by the Nazis. During the war, as Paul-André Comeau explains in his work on the Bloc Populaire,[2] the German propaganda services tried to take advantage of the creation of this nationalist party in 1942, but in vain. Canadians didn't have the pleasure of seeing German U-Boats enter the waters of the St. Lawrence River on a daily basis to deliver agents to local networks of sympathizers, for example!

RUMILLY: A QUEBEC VERSION OF PHILIPPE HENRIOT

It is worth coming back to Robert Rumilly, Jacques de Bernonville's main protector. This historian can be rightly considered to have been the Philippe Henriot of Quebec. He had out-of-the-ordinary intellectual ability, he translated into Quebec terms the very propaganda message the Vichy regime was disseminating in France. One detects Rumilly's prose in Mayor Houde's statements, in Bona Arsenault's flights of rhetoric and even in Justice Cousineau's decision. Rumilly introduced into Quebec such themes as the terrorism of the Resistance, the flaws of the French justice system and the lessons of the French Revolution. Such themes disturbed the average French Canadian, who had been taught by the élite to reject the Republic and who by and large did so with passion. Other intellectuals joined Rumilly and "nationalized" the Bernonville affair, giving the count's defence a force and a credibility which had been missing in Rumilly's crude arguments.

The nationalist position of Rumilly was not modeled on conventional French-Canadian nationalism. The historian had frequented the cafés of Paris and did not believe in the return to the land favoured by his Quebec friends. He even fought for the industrialization of northern Quebec. And in a predominantly Catholic society, Rumilly was not much of a believer. He even admitted having flirted with atheism. Like his master Maurras, he believed that the Church was not very much more than a kind of cement holding society together. Still, the Church was therefore worth supporting. Finally, Rumilly took his dreams for reality when he saw Quebec as an ancien-régime France in America. True enough, the province was steeped in traditions and old-fashioned conservatism, but he was wrong to link Quebec too closely to the medieval France of St. Louis.

What cannot be questioned, however, is that Rumilly was a man of extreme-right-wing convictions. His anti-Semitism, his hatred for Freemasons and Communists, often won out over any other consideration, including sometimes nationalist ones.

Rumilly took advantage of his status as a recognized historian to push the Bernonville affair ahead. He showed a positivist discipline in his serious historical works, but was just beginning to be noticed for his skill as a pamphleteer. He threw himself into the new role of demagogue with ardour. But strangely enough, Rumilly was not representative of the sort of support which Bernonville received in Quebec.

THE FABRICATION OF AN AFFAIR

That is where things stood when the affair was created in Fall 1948. Other collaborators besides Bernonville had slipped into postwar Canada and Quebec. If it hadn't been for Bernonville's rank as a commander rather than an underling like Touvier, events would not have followed the same course. The Canadian authorities certainly did not expect Rumilly to carry out his threats and kick up a fuss in order to keep his friend in Canada. Even within the group of Bernonville supporters, some people, like Hamel, had their doubts about the wisdom of a public campaign. As for Gérard Filion, publisher of *Le Devoir*, he privately blamed Rumilly for exploding a bomb out in the open, although he later conceded that it was an effective course to take.

But on September 5, it was already too late: there was no turning back for Ottawa. The authorities saved something from the wreckage, by quickly ignoring the cases of other collaborators. These latter cases seemed relatively tame when compared to the war criminal Jacques de Bernonville, who had been convicted several times. The government could ease its conscience, because of its handling of the Bernonville affair, while taking pains to ensure that it did not face five or six other similar affairs involving Labedan, Boussat, Huc or Seigneur. These latter collaborators did not have any problems in Canada and enjoyed a peaceful existence on Canadian soil. Over the years, some of them settled permanently in Canada, while others returned to France.

Why was Camillien Houde the standard-bearer in the affair, instead of Adrien Arcand? For one thing, Arcand had lost all credibility by being interned in a Canadian camp during the war. Of course, the same fate had befallen Camillien Houde. But Arcand's professed fascism before the war did not suit the cause of Bernonville, whose defenders did not consider him to be a Nazi.

FOR AND AGAINST

During the Bernonville affair, the hard core of Pétainists in Quebec forged an alliance with very representative nationalists of the "clerico-nationalist" élite. Indeed, the Committee for the Defence of French Political Refugees owed something to both of these movements. There were several kinds of nationalists: former members of the Action Libérale Nationale who had gone over to the Bloc Populaire, where they were subsequently joined by others; a strong contingent of convinced autonomists, card-carrying or members of the party in power in Quebec, the Union Nationale.

These nationalists had good reasons to join Bernonville's defenders. During and after the war, they had been the most ardent supporters of the Marshal. They were genuine Pétainists; that fact, combined with the more typically French-Canadian themes that arose during the affair, starting in October 1948, made it natural for them to offer their support to the campaign.

The nationalists were loud without being very numerous. Their influence particularly in political, cultural, social and religious circles, and the favourable coverage they obtained in the press gave them a lot of prestige. In the paternalist context that still existed in Quebec at the time, they were in a position to shape and mobilize public opinion. The public considered the interests of the élite to be its own interests.

Bernonville profited from the support of the majority of the French-Canadian population once part of its élite asked for help. Does that mean there were three and a half million Pétainists in Quebec? It is true that the Marshal was still highly-regarded at the time. For many people, however, Pétain was little more than a picture blessed by the parish priest and hanging in the presbytery next to portraits of Pius XII and possibly even of de Gaulle. No matter what the strength of Pétainist sympathies, they were enough to give a breathing space to Bernonville in waging his battle against the federal government decision. A kind of diffuse anti-Semitism, combined with conventional anti-Communism, helped tip the scales in favour of the French nobleman.

The Bernonville affair affected the élite, and did not have the same effect on the bulk of the population as the Conscription Crisis did during the war. The only reason that French Canadians poured out their feelings during the affair was the indulgent way the press treated the presumed collaborators.

A vigourous opposition rose up against the élite and the press that supported it, but the opposition had neither the same clout nor the same effect on the public. In French Canada, the movement against Bernonville was led by one newspaper, *Le Canada*, which lacked credibility during the affair since it was controlled by the federal Liberal Party.

It was natural for former members of the French Resistance in Quebec and other veterans to oppose Bernonville. They knew in their bones the difference between collaborators and the Allied forces. These two latter groups acted in the background and gradually moved closer to MPs in Ottawa and anglophone newspapers sympathetic to their cause. It is true that English-language newspapers in Quebec and in the rest of Canada never accepted Bernonville's version of the facts. The disinformation campaign had no effect on anglophone newspapers in Montreal: *The Star*, *The Standard*, *The Herald* and *The Gazette*. There was also silent opposition in Quebec to Bernonville: that of the Jewish community, whose representatives chose to watch the situation and exert discreet pressure on well-known opponents.

The opposition to Bernonville was thus mainly on the other side of the Ottawa River: the CCF, the anglophone press, bureaucrats, some charitable and religious organizations led the campaign, while the Anglo-Canadian public was rather indifferent.

DELIBERATELY DEAF

André Laurendeau, editorialist at *Le Devoir*, invented the expression "deliberately deaf", in his work on the Conscription Crisis. Although it refers to another situation altogether, we mention it here. To explain its meaning, one has first to reply to the question: who knew about Bernonville and what did they know?

From the beginning, the news coming from France about Count de Bernonville forced people to take position. Even before the news reached Quebec, Camellien Houde knew it was coming and got ready. He even launched the disinformation campaign in order to set up a smokescreen and a barricade, to make sure that no other version of the facts could reach and thereby sway public opinion. In order to deform reality in the eyes of the public, Rumilly recognized it was important to have an important public official up-front, such as the mayor of Montreal. Houde provided an extremely useful service.

Once the news arrived in Quebec, the propagandist Rumilly and his allies sifted through it. The French-Canadian press started reporting on the files of the French ministry of the Interior in early September, and those files were very explicit. Rumilly saw the need to discredit both the message and the messenger.

Within a few days, the operation had succeeded. Catholic and nationalist newspapers understood what their public stand should be. They abandoned their critical judgment, and swallowed the doctored version of the facts. Since public figures such as Houde had expressed an opinion, these newspapers accepted that opinion wholeheartedly, as they had already done on other previous occasions.

From this moment onward, the themes Rumilly and his allies had identified were taken up by Roger Duhamel's *Montréal-Matin* and Louis-Philippe Roy's *Action catholique*. Indeed, the same arguments were used by the right-wing press in France.

These ideas had been fabricated by the élite. They were dressed up and served to people who were disposed to accept them. In the minds of the nationalists who joined the committee, the collaborator's crimes were not as significant as what Bernonville represented. It was no time to denounce atrocities. In the culture of the time, the horror of torture could easily be forgotten or subliminated. In postwar Quebec, as in other societies, the question of war crimes was not of particular concern. Besides, the élite relied on newspapers that portrayed only one side of the story. Some were misled. Others allowed themselves to be misled.

It is true that there was not a flood of information about Bernonville. The roadblock thrown up by part of the press meant that the little information there was tended to be published by newspapers opposed to the nationalists, or by the English-language press, which published the French police files about Bernonville.

Among the élite, a consensus was built quite easily. The members of this little society did not seem to want to upset anyone or to risk being ostracized.

In these conditions, the clerico-nationalist élite formed a bloc and did not try to found out any more. Some of its members became deliberately deaf. It was considered good form, in some families, to have an opinion about the Bernonville family without having read the news.

That is why information about Bernonville did not shake the élite or affect the general public. Meanwhile, Liberal and anglophone newspapers smelled a rat. They had no particular sympathy for Pétain, and had a perspective that enabled them to see what was really happening. During the affair, anti-French sentiment did not have the effect on the English-language press that some people claim, although some letters to the editor did link nationalism with fascism.

A RETURN TO THE "TWO SOLITUDES"

The strength of the movement in favour of Bernonville increased dramatically, once it was blended with so-called nationalist issues. André Laurendeau and Gérard Filion at *Le Devoir* were largely responsible for this shift in strategy.

André Laurendeau had not quite shaken off his old sympathies for the Marshal (although he also had sympathy for de Gaulle). At the outset of the affair, Laurendeau announced that he would interpret the story from the nationalist angle. As sensitive, intelligent and experienced as he might have been, Laurendeau did not seem able to rise above culture and generally accepted ideas. Starting in mid-October, he began channeling nationalist energies into the Bernonville affair. His nationalist arguments did not replace appeals in favour of Vichy; they were simply added to them.

As a result, themes such as the flaws of French justice or the control of the French State and justice system by Communists were used side-by-side with such typically nationalist themes as the anti-French prejudice of the anglophone press and bureaucracy and the control of immigration by the Anglo-Saxon majority.

Strictly speaking, and quite apart from the Bernonville affair, the argument about immigration was convincing since it seemed to be well-founded. The anglophone bureaucrats in Ottawa who had decided that Bernonville should be deported thus left themselves open to attack.

There was something cynical in the way the cause was wilfully diverted. French-Canadian organizations did not delve too deeply into the past of a very controversial figure; yet they threw themselves headlong into what they considered to be a new Riel affair. A reader with even an ounce of curiosity and the most rudimentary knowledge of English would have been able to buy a newspaper offering a whole other version of the affair. The fact that the affair solidified around themes reminding French Canadians that they were second-class citizens meant that many people just stopped thinking altogether. The first goal of several nationalist organizations seemed to be simply to make political capital in the name of the French-Canadian identity.

THE LONG SILENCE

The Bernonville affair burst out into the open just when the portents of profound change in Quebec were beginning to appear. A month before the affair broke in the newspapers, the manifesto *Refus global* came out. It gave an indication of things to come. The following year, the dramatic strike in the mining town of Asbestos came to a conclusion. In 1950, the review *Cité libre* was created, and threw a challenge to traditionalist nationalism. Finally, the death of Pétain in 1951 weakened French-Canadian solidarity with the nostalgic Pétainists of France and their ideological cause.

Moreover, the élite in Quebec quickly appreciated that a new cultural and social climate was in the making, one very different from the climate which had allowed them to justify their refusal to believe the truth about Bernonville's past. The remnants of the Thirties and Forties quickly vanished.

In this new situation, and with incontrovertible information in hand about Bernonville's collaboration, the élite had a hard time facing reality. It was like waking up from a nightmare. Some people even asked how they could possibly have sought to support Bernonville. Others simply changed sides. The same thing happened with their support for Pétain. The Vichy syndrome set in motion in Quebec. Long-standing support for Pétain and for Bernonville was covered up and forgotten.

In *Le syndrome de Vichy*, the historian Henri Rousso brilliantly demonstrates how the years of the Occupation were downplayed in postwar France.[3] His book is very revealing. Rousso examines how, from 1944 to the present, the collective memory of France has had to accommodate painful memories associated with the 1940-1944 period, when the Vichy régime operated in the southern zone. He reveals the continuing mourning, the repression of memories, the silences.... On a different scale, this Vichy syndrome can also be applied to Quebec.

As soon as Bernonville left, the affair vanished. Nobody dared speak about it again. In Fall 1951, the French ambassador sought to justify the position which had been taken by France's Quebec cousins.

Some of them, he claimed, did not withdraw their support once they had offered it, and only realized when it was too late that the story told by Bernonville was improbable. The ambassador's overtures did not get people talking. People preferred to remain silent. The disintegration of the movement supporting Pétain and Bernonville was swallowed up in the collective memory. The Quiet Revolution, an important renewal of Quebec society in the early Sixties, had a big effect as well. Amnesia and indulgent silence meant that the Bernonville affair simply vanished, and was not even alluded to in the political memoirs of René Chaloult.

When Canon Lionel Groulx published his ponderous memoirs in the early 1970s (which he had actually started writing in the 1950s), he did not even mention Quebec support for Pétain. When André Laurendeau came to write about Quebec support for Pétain in his book on the Conscription Crisis, he wrote the story of this support at a 20-year distance.

The dramatic content of this story should not be ignored. The episode can actually serve to stimulate historical research in order to clarify whole periods of Quebec history which have been repressed in the collective memory. The Bernonville affair could also be used in comparative studies still to come, to assess the support Canada's Italian and Ukrainian communities gave to people of the same origin who were suspected of war crimes or of collaboration. Fascinating avenues of research are opening up for historians.

FOOTNOTES

1. Francis Arzalier, *Les perdants: la dérive fasciste des mouvements autonomiste et indépendantiste au XXe siècle*, Paris, La Découverte, 1990.

2. Paul-André Comeau, *Le Bloc populaire, 1942-1948*, Montreal, Québec/Amérique, 1982.

3. Henri Rousso, *Le syndrome de Vichy de 1944 à nos jours*, Paris, Seuil, 1987.

CHRONOLOGY

October 23, 1897	Birth in Fort-de-France (Martinique) of Robert Rumilly
December 20, 1897	Birth in Paris of Jacques Dugé de Bernonville
1928	Robert Rumilly left France for Canada
September 10, 1939	Canada declared war on Germany

1940

May	The police arrested leading Canadian Fascists, among them Adrien Arcand, who was interned from 1940 to 1945.
June 18	General de Gaulle's appeal to France on the BBC.
July 10	Vichy's National Assembly accorded all powers to the Pétain government. The latter became "Chief of State" on July 11.
August 1	General de Gaulle's appeal to French Canada.

1942

April 27	Plebiscite: with a 71.2% vote, Quebec refused to free the Liberal government of its promise concerning military service. The eight other provinces were 80% in favour, however.
August 18-19	French Canadians participated in the disastrous raid on Dieppe
October	The League for the Defence of Canada, a group hostile to the war,became a political movement under the name Bloc Populaire Canadien.
November 27	Toulon was occupied. The French fleet was scuttled.

1943

January 31	The Légion du service d'ordre légionnaire (SOL) became the Milice.
Fall	Bernonville took an oath to Hitler and appeared on the German payroll.

1944

January	Darnand was appointed at the head of the Maintenance of Order in Vichy.
March 26	The Germans, supported by some *Milice* units, attacked 465 Maquis fighters on the Glières plâteau
April 15	Under the command of Dagostini and Bernonville, the Milice took repressive measures in the Vercors region.
April 28	Pétain declared that the Resistance was compromising the future of the country.
May and June	Repressions operations led by Bernonville in Saône-et-Loire.
June 6	Allied D-Day landings in Normandy.

June 29	Assassination in Rillieux-la-Pape, near Lyon, of seven Jews by Paul Touvier's men.
July 11-13	General de Gaulle's visit to Quebec.
July 20-21	The German army wiped out the Maquis fighters in the Vercors region.
August 5	Pétain solemnly condemned the actions of the Milice.
August 20	Bernonville fled to Germany in the company of high-ranking Nazi officers.
August 24	General de Gaulle entered Paris.
Fall	Bernonville was parachuted behind Allied lines in France on an Axis sabotage mission.

1945

| End of April | René Lévesque, war correspondent with the 7th Army of the American general Patch, was one of the first to enter Dachau. |
| November | Marshal Pétain was interned on Ile d'Yeu. |

1946

June 14	The milicien Jean Louis Huc arrived in Sorel, with false papers
July 13	Julien Labedan left France for Canada.
September	Arrival in Canada of Georges Montel.
November	Arrival of Jacques de Bernonville in Canada, by train from New York

1947

| October 8 | The Toulouse court of justice sentenced Jacques Dugé de Bernonville to death. |
| Mid-December | Bernonville was recognized and photographed in Granby. |

1948

Mid-January	Bernonville and his family reported to Immigration offices in Montreal to request a permanent residency permit.
January 21	Inauguration of the fleur-de-lis flag as Quebec's official flag.
February	Montel received an expulsion order from Canadian immigration authorities.
May	Montel's order is suspended.
August	Publication of the manifesto *Refus global*.
September 2	Bernonville and his family detained by the Immigration authorities in Montreal.
September 3	Houde intervened and got in touch with the press in order to save Bernonville.
September 10	The Committee for the Defence of French Political Refugees was created in Montreal.

September 22

Order-in-council passed, allowing four Frenchmen
to remain in Canada; Bernonville was not among them.

October 15

The presence of four other French collaborators
was revealed in the newspapers.

1949
February 21

Justice Cousineau recommended that federal authorities
grant Bernonville the right to remain in Canada.
The federal government order Immigration authorities
to undertake a second inqruiy into the Bernonville file.

July

End of thehistoric asbestos strike.

1950
February 16

New expulsion and deportation order for Bernonville.

April 17

Well-known French-Canadian public figures signed
a petition supporting Bernonville.

1951
January 5

Amnesty law in France

July 23

Death of Marshal Pétain, at the age of 95.

August 17

Bernonville departed suddenly for Brazil.

1952-1994
1952

French authorities requested that Brazil extradite
Jacques de Bernonville.

October 1956

The federal Supreme Court of Brazil rejected the
French embassy's request for Bernonville's extradition.

November 23, 1971

French President Georges Pompidou pardoned Paul Touvier.

April 27, 1972

Jacques de Bernonville was assassinated in Brazil.

March 8, 1983

Robert Rumilly died, at the age of 85.

July 4, 1987

Klaus Barbie was sentenced to life imprisonment.

April 20, 1994

Paul Touvier was sentenced to life imprisonment
for to crimes against humanity.

BIBLIOGRAPHY

ARCHIVES AND DOCUMENTS

1. Rumilly Collection

The essential documents on the Bernonville affair are to be found in the Robert Rumilly Collection, which was transferred in two stages to the Archives nationales du Québec in Montreal. The last and most signficant transfer was made in February 1992. The 38 boxes in this last transfer have not been systematically catalogued. They are largely thrown together in six boxes, and there are some 1,220 documents concerning the Bernonville affair.

The interest of this collection resides in its wealth. It seems Rumilly never threw out a single letter, and kept them for posterity without informing his correspondents he was doing so. Sometimes, he went so far as to type out handwritten letters he had received. The historian also had the habit of always keeping one or even several copies of his own letters. Finally, throughout the Bernonville affair, he made a point of keeping any document from any protagonist in the affair. The collection also contains a wealth of press clippings on Bernonville's difficulties in Canada.

2. Louis Saint-Laurent Collection

Correspondence sent to Prime Minister Louis Saint-Laurent concerning the Bernonville affair was included in the Louis Saint-Laurent Collection transferred to the National Archives of Canada. These documents throw light on the real knowledge Saint-Laurent had of count de Bernonville's past. They also reveal that Saint-Laurent's only concern during the affair was to avoid political problems.

3. Bernonville Collection

Another 500 pages on Jacques de Bernonville can also be found at the National Archives of Canada. They consist mostly of photocopies of documents generated during Immigration inquiries into Bernonville's real past. These documents, some of which have been heavily censored, indicate clearly that government officials quickly found out about Bernonville's collaborationist past.

4. Archives of the Canadian Jewish Congress

Some 30 documents concerning the Bernonville affair are kept in the Canadian Jewish Congress Archives in Montreal. They are particularly interesting in that they show how members of the Jewish community viewed the French-Canadian press of the time. Moreover, correspondence between the CJC and the Conseil représentatif des Juifs de France shows that French Jews were far harsher about French Canadians than Jews in Canada.

4. Simon Wiesenthal Centre

In Toronto, Sol Littman of the Simon Wiesenthal Centre on war criminals built up an exhaustive dossier on Jacques de Bernonville. Other interesting Free French documents about Bernonville can also be found in Toronto.

6. Archives of the Foreign Affairs Ministry of France

Some members of the French diplomatic corps in Ottawa and Montreal played an important role in the Bernonville affair. However, neither the embassy in Ottawa nor the consulate in Montreal have any archival material on the subject. If there is any file on Jacques de Bernonville at the Foreign Affairs Ministry of France, we have been told, then it will only become accessible 100 years after the last extradition proceedings ended.

BRIEF BIBLIOGRAPHY

A. French period

ARON, R., *Histoire de la libération de la France, juin 1944-mai 1945*, Ottawa, Cercle du livre de France, 1959.

ARON, R., *Histoire de l'épuration*, Paris, Fayard, vol. 1, 1967.

ARZALIER, F., *Les perdants: la dérive fasciste des mouvement autonomistes et indépendantistes au XXe siècle*, Paris, La Découverte, 1990.

AZÉMA, J.-P., *De Munich à la Libération*, Paris, Seuil, 1979.

AZÉMA, J.-P. and F. BÉDARIDA, *Vichy et les Français*, Paris, Fayard, 1992.

BAYAC, J. Delpierré de, *Histoire de la Milice (1918-1945)*, Paris, Fayard, 1969 (Réédité chez Fayard, 1994).

BERNADAC, C. *"Dagore", les carnets secrets de la Cagoule*, Paris, Éditions France-Empire, 1977.

DELARUE, J., *Histoire de la Gestapo*, Paris, Fayard, 1970.

FERRO, M., *Questions sur la IIe Guerre mondiale*, Florence, Casterman/Giunti, 1993.

HOOVER INSTITUTION ON WAR, REVOLUTION AND PEACE, *France during the German Occupation*, Stanford (California), vol. 1, 1958.

KASPI, A., *Les Juifs pendant l'Occupation*, Paris, Seuil, 1991.

LACOUTURE, J., *De Gaulle*, Paris, Seuil, 3 vols., 1983-1986.

LOTTMAN, H., *L'épuration*, Paris, Fayard/Seuil, 1986.

MILZA, P., and S. BERSTEIN, *Dictionnaire historique des fascismes et du nazisme*, Brussels, Éditions Complexe, 1992.

NOGUÈRES, H., *Histoire de la résistance en France*, Paris, Robert Laffont, vol. III, 1972.

ORY, P. *Les collaborateurs, 1940-1945*, Paris, Seuil, 1977.

PARIS, E., *L'affaire Barbie: analyse d'un mal français*, Paris, Ramsay, 1985.

PAXTON, R.O., *La France de Vichy, 1940-1944*, Paris, Seuil, 1973.

RÉMOND, R. (ed.) *Paul Touvier et l'Église*, Paris, Fayard, 1992.

ROUSSO, H., *Pétain et la fin de la collaboration*, Brussels, Éditions Complexe, MA Éditions, 1984.

ROUSSO, H., *La collaboration*, Paris, MA Éditions, 1987.

ROUSSO, H. *Le syndrome de Vichy de 1944 à nos jours*, Paris, Seuil, 1987.

B. Quebec period

ABELLA, I. and H. TROPER, *None is too many*, Toronto, Lester and Orpend Dennys, 1983.

ANCTIL, P., *"Le Devoir", les Juifs et l'immigration, De Bourassa à Laurendeau*, Quebec, Institut québécois de recherche sur la culture, 1988.

ANCTIL, P. and G. CALDWELL, *Juifs et réalités juives au Québec*, Quebec, Institut québécois de recherche sur la culture, 1984.

BEAULIEU, A., J. HAMELIN, et al. *La presse québécoise des origines à nos jours*, Sainte Foy, Presses de l'Université Laval, volumes IV to VII, 1979-1985.

BLACK, C., *Duplessis*, Toronto, McClelland and Stewart, 1977.

CHALOULT, R., *Mémoires politiques*, Montreal, Fides 1969.

COMEAU, P.-A., *Le Bloc populaire, 1942-48*, Montreal, Québec/Amérique, 1982.

COMEAU, R. and L. BEAUDRY, *André Laurendeau, un intellectuel d'ici*, Sillery, Presses de l'Université du Québec, 1990.

DELISLE, E., *Le traître et le juif*, Outremont, L'Étincelle éditeur, 1992.

DESCHÊNES COMMISSION, *Report of the Commission of inquiry on war crimes*, Ottawa, Supply and Services Canada, 1986.

DION, L., *Québec 1945-2000*, vol. 2: *Les intellectuels et le temps de Duplessis*, Sainte Foy, Presses de l'Université Laval, 1993.

GOUGEON, G., *Histoire du nationalisme québécois*, Montreal, VLB éditeur/SRC, 1993.

GROULX, L., *Mes mémoires*, Montreal, Fidès, vol I to IV, 1972-1974.

LAURENDEAU, A., *La crise de la conscription, 1942*, Montreal, Éditions du Jour, 1962.

LINTEAU, P.-A. et al, *Histoire du Québec contemporain*, vol. II: *Le Québec depuis 1930*, Montreal, Boréal, 1986.

LITTMAN, S., *War Criminal on Trial: the Rauca Case*, Toronto, Lester and Orpen Dennys, 1983.

MALAVOY, A., *La mort attendra*, Montreal, Éditions de l'Homme, 1961.

MIRIBEL, É. de, *La liberté souffre violence*, Paris, Plon, 1981.

MONIÈRE, D., *André Laurendeau et le destin d'un peuple*, Montreal, Québec/Amérique, 1983.

PICKERSGILL, J.W., *Louis Saint Laurent*, Outremont, Lidec, 1983.

PROVENCHER, J., *Chronologie du Québec*, Montreal, Boréal, 1991.

RUMILLY, R., *Histoire de la Société Saint-Jean-Baptiste de Montréal*, Montreal, L'Aurore, 1975.

THOMSON, D.-C., *De Gaulle et le Québec*, Saint Laurent, Éditions du Trécarré, 1990.

TRUDEL, M., *Mémoires d'un autre siècle*, Montreal, Boréal, 1987.

WADE, M. *The French Canadians from 1760 to 1967*, Toronto, MacMillan, 1968.